The
Wind Birds

THE CURIOUS NATURALIST

The
WindBirds

Shorebirds of North America

BY PETER MATTHIESSEN
Cover painting by Robert Verity Clem
Illustrations by Robert Gillmor

CHAPTERS™

CHAPTERS PUBLISHING LTD., SHELBURNE, VERMONT 05482

Published by
Chapters Publishing Ltd.
2031 Shelburne Road
Shelburne, Vermont 05482

The text by Peter Matthiessen was originally published in 1967, in different form, in *The Shorebirds of North America*, Gardner D. Stout, ed., The Viking Press. The second edition was published as *The Wind Birds* in 1973 by The Viking Press, Inc.

Library of Congress Cataloging-in-Publication Data
Matthiessen, Peter.
    The wind birds / by Peter Matthiessen ; illustrations by Robert Gillmor.
        p.   cm. — (The Curious naturalist series)
    Originally published : New York : Viking Press, 1973.
    Includes bibliographical references (p.   ) and index.
    ISBN 1-881527-37-9 (paper) : $12.95
    1. Shore birds—Behavior.   I. Gillmor , Robert.   II. Title
    III. Series.
    QL698.3.M37   1994
    598.3 ' 3—dc20   93-48005

Trade distribution by Firefly Books Ltd.
250 Sparks Avenue, Willowdale, Ontario, Canada M2H 2S4

Printed and bound in Canada by Friesen Printers, Altona, Manitoba

Most of the text originally appeared in *The New Yorker*.

Grateful acknowledgment is made to the following for permission to quote copyrighted material:
    Doubleday & Company, Inc.: From *An Introduction to Haiku* by Harold G. Henderson. Copyright © 1958 by Harold G. Henderson. Reprinted by permission.
    The Macmillan Company (New York), Macmillan & Co. Ltd. (London), and Mr. M. B. Yeats for "Paudeen" (page 17) from *Collected Poems* by W. B. Yeats. Copyright 1916 by The Macmillan Company, renewed 1944 by Bertha Georgie Yeats.
    New Directions Publishing Corporation, J. M. Dent & Sons Ltd., and the Trustees for the Copyrights of the late Dylan Thomas for "In the White Giant's Thigh" (page 141) from *The Collected Poems of Dylan Thomas*. Copyright 1953 by Dylan Thomas.
    The Viking Press, Inc., for lines from *The Fables of La Fontaine* (page 65), translated by Marianne Moore. Copyright 1954 by Marianne Moore.

Designed by Hans Teensma / Impress, Inc.,

Cover art: American Avocet (shown with Phalaropes) painted by Robert Verity Clem, from the collection of the Library of the Academy of Natural Sciences, Philadelphia

For Mary Matthiessen Wheelwright

Acknowledgments

I am grateful, first of all, to field ornithologist Kevin Zimmer for contributing a foreword that describes the evolution of shorebird study since the first publication of this book. In that edition, Dr. Ralph S. Palmer and also John Bull of the American Museum of Natural History reviewed the original manuscript in its entirety, and there is scarcely a page that did not benefit from corrections or observations by one or both. More recently, Dr. George M. Sutton drew attention to certain errors, and later Dr. David F. Parmelee checked the entire text, making additional corrections and suggestions. None of these authorities are responsible for any errors that may remain, much less for speculation by myself or others.

Speculation (so long as it is so identified) is essential to the purpose of this book, which is an essay on the shorebirds of North America but also a general introduction—using the shorebirds as illustration—to the study of comparative behavior. Because it is general and broad in its aim, I have not crippled my account with the innumerable qualifications, opposing views, long footnotes and supporting citations that would be required were all specialists to be satisfied. The sources of direct quotations as well as of obscure or disputed ideas may be found in the Selected Bibliography. For the rest, I can only say that reputable authority has been found for every statistic, statement and idea that is not clearly presented as my own observation or opinion.

Much of the material on bird biology and general behavior was drawn from Joel Welty's excellent *The Life of Birds*, and many illustrations of shorebird behavior were derived, inevitably, from Arthur Cleveland Bent, whose mighty *Life Histories of North American Shorebirds* remains the standard reference work on North American birds. Remarks on evolution and genetics and speciation are based primarily on the work of Ernst Mayr, and illustrations of comparative behavior were taken freely from E. A. Armstrong, M. M. Nice, Niko Tinbergen and many others (see Selected

Bibliography). My own ideas and observations, scattered here and there throughout, are offered with neither assurance nor apology. If one of these should provoke somebody to prove or disprove it, we will know something that we did not know before, and the book will have served its purpose.

—P. M.

Foreword

The reprinting of *The Wind Birds* is a most happy publishing event, not only because the book fanned my own flames of curiosity 20 years ago, but because it is a timeless piece of writing that will continue to inform, inspire and captivate students of animal behavior, shorebird enthusiasts and lovers of nature for generations to come.

It wasn't until autumn of my first year of birding, at the age of 14, that shorebirds took a firm hold on my consciousness. A land-locked existence in eastern North Dakota offered no beaches or estuaries for my brother and me to prowl, and although we did see some shorebirds during the course of the summer, those encounters were not particularly enlightening.

Then an article appeared in the newspaper, written by a local birder, detailing the avian riches found during migration periods at the settling ponds owned by the local sugarbeet-refining company. We prevailed upon our parents for a ride out to the ponds, which were hidden from the road by tall, brush-covered dikes. As we made our way over the embankment, we saw a series of six "ponds," some of them more mud than water. The shorelines in the corners of these ponds were alive with birds—shorebirds, tracing zigzag patterns of tiny footprints in the muddy effluent.

The afternoon sun was low in the sky, and the quality of our binoculars was lower still, but over the next two hours we became completely absorbed in the actions of the birds before us—flocks of plump dowitchers feeding in the mud, noisy yellowlegs pacing along the shore and twittering peeps dashing here and there. Given our inexperience and the limitations of our optics, the smaller birds were maddeningly difficult to identify. But above all, I remember being overwhelmed by the mystery of these birds, who in their calls and movements seemed to share some higher form of interspecific communication. Border skirmishes were frequent but brief among the different species feeding side by side, and when a harrier made periodic passes over the pond, all of the shorebirds would burst into flight with an unusual singularity of purpose, separate into their respective groups and then proceed to give a stunning demonstration of synchronized evasive flying before settling again in their original spots.

I left the sugarbeet ponds that day hopelessly enamored of shorebirds, and hungering to learn more about them. Unfortunately, most books contain only dry accounts of identification features or behavior and little that captures the essence of these magical birds. Finally, I found what I was looking for in *The Wind Birds*. Here, at last, is an author who makes sense of the behavioral intricacies of the shorebirds without dulling the romance and wonder they inspire in those who watch them.

One cannot read *The Wind Birds* without feeling a certain sadness, for within its pages, Matthiessen details the rampant market gunning of the last century that decimated shorebird flocks and nearly drove several species to extinction. In the 1960s, species such as the Hudsonian godwit seemed precarious in status, having rebounded only slightly from previous population lows. Happily, however, in the last 20 years, depleted shorebird populations have continued to recover, and while the skies will never again be darkened by clouds of shorebirds as in previous centuries, most species are at least maintaining healthy population levels. This past June I witnessed a gathering of more than 200 Hudsonian godwits on the mudflats of Turnagain Arm in Anchorage, Alaska, a concentration that would have been unthinkable just 30 years ago. While Hudsonian godwits are still seen in relatively small numbers along the East Coast each fall, we now know this is because they migrate non-stop for thousands of miles, rather than because they are rare.

This is not to imply that the "wind birds" are secure, for new threats to their existence have arisen. Recent work has revealed that many species mass in staggering concentrations each year at a few widely scattered points along their migration routes. These staging areas provide predictable concentrations of superabundant food resources, where famished birds can refuel quickly prior to, or in the midpoints of, their protracted and arduous journeys. In the course of a few weeks, such spots may host more than three-quarters of the entire continental population of some species, creating bottlenecks at which even abundant species may be vulnerable to disaster. Encroachment of human development at these sites, as well as the ever-present dangers of oil and chemical spills, represent real threats to the future of many species.

Nowhere is this phenomenon of shorebird staging with its attendant dangers better illustrated than at Delaware Bay, where more than one million shorebirds (primarily red knots and ruddy turnstones) annually synchronize their northbound migration to coincide with the spawning of the horseshoe crabs, on whose eggs they feed. Coastal development forced shorebird concentrations into increasingly smaller areas until the government intervened and established protected reserves. Many such staging sites have been identified and protected in North America, but this alone is not sufficient to ensure the continued health of shorebird populations. Similar staging areas exist along both coasts of Central and South America, and even one weak link in the precarious chain could be disasterous. Fortunately, international coalitions of researchers and conservation organizations are aggressively attempting to identify and protect sites critical to migratory shorebirds.

Disrupting their long-established migratory paths is not all that threatens the shorebirds. Rampant draining of prairie wetlands could ultimately threaten some of the more southerly breeders, and increasing pressure to open more of the Arctic to oil exploration and development could have long-reaching effects on many species. The extensive conversion of native short-grass prairie to agricultural land has already produced a severe downward spiral in the number of mountain plovers, and similar conversion of other grasslands may be destructive to the populations of upland sandpipers and long-billed curlews.

In the last 20 years, the increasing popularity of birding has led to a continuing revolution in the area of field identification of all birds, and shorebirds are no exception. A better understanding of molt cycles and attention to the fine details of plumage have yielded discoveries about field marks that allow the field separation of many species pairs once thought inseparable (among them long-billed versus short-billed dowitchers, western versus semi-palmated sandpipers and rufous-necked versus little stints). Now, entire books are devoted solely to shorebird identification.

With ever-increasing numbers of avid observers, all armed with superior optics and a more sophisticated knowledge of field marks, it is only natural that the number of vagrant shorebird sightings in North America would increase. Such rarities as ruffs, curlew sandpipers and little and rufous-necked stints are turning up on the Atlantic Coast with increasing frequency, and the West Coast has hosted a parade of long-distance vagrants, from little curlews to great knots. Intensive coverage of the outer Aleutians and other Alaskan outposts has revealed that many of these Eurasian wanderers are regular in their occurrence, and some are even known to occur in numbers each year.

The identification revolution has not been accompanied by a taxonomic revolution. In fact, shorebird taxonomy, at least of North American species, has remained very stable over the last 20 years. The only major change has been the recent recognition that the various forms of golden plovers are specifically distinct. Shorebird enthusiasts must now sort out the Pacific golden plover (*Pluvialis fulva*), which nests in western and northern Alaska and migrates both over the open Pacific as well as along the Pacific coast, from the American golden plover (*P. dominica*), which nests across the Canadian and Alaskan arctic and subarctic and migrates from one coast to the other, from the greater golden plover (*P. apricaria*), which reaches our shores only as a rare vagrant to the Maritime Provinces of Canada.

Much of the shorebird research conducted in the last two decades has centered on the evolution of mating systems. As Peter Matthiessen details in this book, shorebirds as a family display a wide range of mating habits, from monogamy to polygyny, polyandry, promiscuity and nearly everything in between. Indeed, shorebirds such as the jaçana, phalarope and spotted sandpiper are the basis of much of what we know of polyandry (a system in which females establish pair bonds with multiple males) in birds. Other shorebird species whose mating systems may differ from one pair to the next have been theorized to be intermediate links in the evolutionary development of polyandry and other systems. Earlier ecological work focused on identifying and describing the types of mating systems employed by various species. Current work is aimed toward pinpointing the evolutionary basis for divergent mating systems.

In spite of the attention now being paid to the shorebirds, mysteries remain. The first nest of the bristle-thighed curlew was found in Alaska as recently as 1948, and it is only in the last several years that the known nesting range has been expanded to include several areas in the Seward Peninsula. The eskimo curlew remains shrouded in mystery and intrigue. Reported sightings are frequent, but photographic documentation has remained minimal. Among the birding community, conspiracy theories abound, with rumors of known Canadian breeding sites whose locations are being kept secret by governmental wildlife agencies. Likewise, word of verified sightings in the historic wintering grounds in South America has filtered our way in the last two years. We can only hope that a few survivors of this genetic lineage do indeed still safely navigate the journey from arctic Canada to Argentina.

Wonder and mystery will always accompany the shorebirds. Just as their arrival in spring heralds a timeless sense of renewal, so does their passage in fall evoke a certain sad nostalgia for simpler times, for barefoot days on the beaches of our youth. Let us hope that people will always recognize the intrinsic value of shorebirds, and that appropriate actions will be taken to ensure that future generations will feel the same joy in the spring song of the upland sandpiper or the pangs of melancholy in the curlew's sad cry.

—*Kevin J. Zimmer*

Is it really worth while to spend our time, the time which escapes us so swiftly, this stuff of life, as Montaigne calls it, in gleaning facts of indifferent moment and highly contestable utility? Is it not childish to inquire so minutely into an insect's actions? Too many interests of a graver kind hold us in their grasp to leave leisure for these amusements. That is how the harsh experience of age impels us to speak; that is how I should conclude . . . if I did not perceive, amid the chaos of my observations, a few gleams of light toughing the loftiest problems which we are privileged to discuss . . . . What is life? Will it ever be possible for us to trace its sources? What is human intelligence? What is instinct? . . . These questions are and always will be the despair of every cultivated mind, even though the insanity of our efforts to solve them urges us to cast them into the limbo of the unknowable.

—J. Henri Fabre

HUDSONIAN GODWIT

I

. . . I stumbled blind
Among the stones and thorn-trees, under morning light;
Until a curlew cried and in the luminous wind
A curlew answered; and suddenly thereupon I thought
That on the lonely height where all are in God's eye,
There cannot be, confusion of our sound forgot,
A single soul that lacks a sweet crystalline cry.

—*W. B. Yeats,* "Paudeen"

THE POND at Sagaponack, where I live, has its source in the small woodland stream which drains Poxabogue Pond and Little Poxabogue, further inland. From the west windows of my house, a fringe of trees parting the fields winds into view; here Sagg Pond, like a wide meadow river, curls down through miles of warm potato country to the sea. The Long Island farmland fills the landscape to the north and west and spreads toward the southward; Sagg Pond appears again, turned back upon itself by the hard white of the dunes, by the hard blue of the sea horizon. The pond bends like the shank of a great hook; it is now a mile across. But seasonally, in storm or flood, the pond is open to the sea. Then this lower reach is salt, a place of tidal creek and shallow flat which is today, as it has always been, a haunt of shorebirds.

On the fourth of July of 1870, a Boston gentleman, George H. Mackay, killed 27 woodcock at "Poxybang Pond"; a few days later, 39 "dowitch" were gently slain at Sagaponack. The woodcock still comes to Poxabogue and the dowitcher to Sagaponack, though the dowitcher—its odd name may derive from "Deutscher snipe," due to its popularity, in Revolutionary times, among the Hessians—is now protected legally from guns, a circumstance which Mr. Mackay, one of the rare naturalist-sports-men in an epoch of mighty game hogs, would doubtless find astonishing. Mackay and his contemporaries pursued the shorebirds with such vigor that when he died, in 1928, the hosts that flew down the long seacoasts of his youth had been reduced to fugitive small bands.

On September 28 of 1964, after a day and night of onshore winds, a flock of 68 golden plover pitched into the potato field between my house and Sagaponack Pond; in that small flock at Sagaponack there flew more golden plover than the total I had seen in 20 years. Yet Audubon once re-ported a flight of "millions" of golden plover near New Orleans, of which some 48,000 were killed in a single day: The golden plover is thought[32*] to have been even more numerous than the Eskimo curlew, whose multi-tudes have been compared to the great flights of the passenger pigeon. From colonial times, plover and curlew had been hunted in spring and fall, but they suffered no fatal diminishment until the last part of the nineteenth century when, with the fading of the wild pigeon, the market guns were turned upon shorebirds and waterfowl. Even the least sand-piper met a violent end when the larger species were in short supply, though its minuscule roast would scarcely make a mouthful, bones and all: in one account,[8] 97 of these "ox-eyes" were cut down with a single shot.

But the plover and curlew were the favorite birds, not only because of their great numbers and fine taste but because they were unsuspicious to a fault. The Eskimo curlew would circle back over the guns, calling out to

---

* Superscript figures refer to the numbers in the Selected Bibliography, page 153.

its fallen companions, a habit it shared with the dunlin, dowitcher and many others. That the dunlin was called the "simpleton" on Long Island indicates the low esteem in which its brain was held (the piping plover was known as the "feeble" and the willet as the "humility," but the plover's name is derived from its call, and that of the willet from a family trait of feeding in the "humble mud"), and the buff-breasted and solitary sandpipers were celebrated far and wide for stubborn innocence. (Dr. Elliott Coues, taking advantage of a rare convention of solitary sand-pipers, once collected seven of this species, shooting one at a time, before the eighth and last, suspecting that something was amiss, took leave—"I will add in justice to his wits," wrote Dr. Coues, "in a great hurry."[22]

Under the circumstances, one wonders that any shorebirds survived into the present century. Not only were they trapped and shot, but great numbers of knots and other species were taken by "fire-lighting," a noc-turnal practice much in favor on Long Island's Great South Bay and else-where, in which the resting flocks, blinded but undismayed by a bright beam, stood by while market men stepped forth from punts and wrung their necks. Night hunting took such a toll of a then-common source of public nourishment that Massachusetts in 1835 passed a law forbidding the take of "Plover, Curlew, Dough-bird, and Chicken-bird" after dark: the dough-bird was the Eskimo curlew, and the chicken-bird was the ruddy turnstone.

A decade later, Rhode Island passed a law forbidding spring shooting of woodcock and snipe, but this admirable and precocious measure on behalf of the two species which least needed it was repealed in the face of public outrage, and for the next 70 years almost nothing was done to slow the destruction of the shorebirds, whose narrow migration paths, close-flocking habits and chronic foolishness contributed heavily to their own decline.

By the turn of the century, George Mackay was growing concerned about the shorebirds, which were rapidly disappearing from his hunting circuit. Mackay's notes[54] on the fall migrations of the Eskimo curlew and golden plover for the years from 1896 to 1899 are among the first warn-ings we have of the curlew's rapid disappearance, even though a "fute" at

Montauk in 1891 was the last of this species ever seen on Long Island (four were reported at Montauk in September of 1932, but the sighting is not generally accepted), and in New England, after 1897, no more than three were seen again in a single flock. In that same year, Mackay inquired publicly: "Are we not approaching the beginning of the end?"[55] though his private journal reveals that he was still blazing away at shorebirds of all descriptions and was out before dawn in vain pursuit of the very bird whose passing he so lamented. "Although hopeless," he writes, "I was driving over the western plover ground at daylight, hoping to find a few tired birds."[56] In this period, "fire-lighted" knots still sold in Boston for ten cents a dozen.

Whether uneasy or discouraged at the meager sport, Mackay did little hunting after 1897, and later he was to lead campaigns against spring shooting. But in 1916, at a time when the golden plover was fast following the Eskimo curlew toward oblivion, Mackay and his party "succeeded in shooting" one forlorn specimen at Nantucket where, a half-century before, both curlew and plover had appeared in such waves as to "almost darken the sun."[32] And he was still at it in October of 1921, flanked now by younger generations of Mackays. "We saw in all eight Black-breast plovers, young birds, and I shot four. On picking them up, one proved to be a young Golden plover (pale-belly). If I could have a little practice I feel I could come back to my old shooting form fairly well."[56] One feels a reluctant affection for this doughty old gentleman—he was then very close to 80—who led in the public fight for the protection of the shorebirds without once questioning his private right to kill them.

George Mackay's last shorebird, a ruddy turnstone, was shot illegally in 1922; the species had come under the protection of the Federal Migratory Bird Treaty Act four years earlier. Within the decade, all shorebirds except the snipe and woodcock had been removed from the list of game birds. But the Eskimo curlew had already passed the point of no return (though it has made a miraculous reappearance every time it has been mourned and buried; two Eskimo curlews were reported at Galveston Island, Texas, as recently as 1963, and a solitary specimen, in September of the same year, was shot by a hunter in Barbados), and the

Hudsonian godwit and buff-breasted sandpiper, the long-billed curlew and golden plover are nowhere plentiful. Probably these species will remain uncommon, for their breeding and wintering grounds in both Americas are evermore threatened by man, but they are no longer fluttering at the edge of the abyss. Even the stilt sandpiper, never abundant, was recently reported[6] in Saskatchewan in a flight estimated at 4,000.

The Eskimo curlew excepted, the Hudsonian godwit is the one North American shorebird whose future still seems uncertain. In 1926 hope for the species had been all but abandoned. ("The passing of this bird must be a cause for regret among sportsmen and nature lovers alike . . ."[110]) A decade later, the godwit had almost vanished. In recent years it has recuperated and is even common here and there in spring in the Mississippi Valley, but the flock of 24 that I watched (with Robert Clem) one misty August afternoon in 1963 on the salt flats of Monomoy Island, south of Cape Cod, represented a large percentage of the Hudsonian godwits that still occur on the coasts of the Atlantic in the fall: except for a solitary bird that came one Indian summer to Sagaponack, they were the only Hudsonian godwits I have ever seen.

The last entry of Mackay's Shooting Journal, for August 16 of 1922, concludes as follows:

> At noon we picked up and went up to the house on Third Point, where we had dinner, Bunt having dug a bucket of clams. As usual we had a strong S.W. breeze to return with. The day was fine but very hot.[56]

And we close the book with the warm breath of summer tide flats in our nostrils and a vague longing for those blue-and-golden days when the great bird companies that no man will see again flew *south* along the line of surf and vanished into the ocean mists.

The restlessness of shorebirds, their kinship with the distance and swift seasons, the wistful signal of their voices down the long coastlines of the world make them, for me, the most affecting of wild creatures. I think of them as birds of wind, as "wind birds." To the traveler confounded by exotic birds, not to speak of exotic specimens of his own kind, the voice of the wind birds may be the lone familiar note in a strange land, and I have many times been glad to find them; meeting a whimbrel one fine summer day of February in Tierra del Fuego, I wondered if I had not seen this very bird a half-year earlier, at home. The spotted and white-rumped sandpipers, the black-bellied and golden plovers are birds of Sagaponack, but the spotted sandpiper has cheered me with its jaunty teeter on the Amazon and high up in the Andes (and so has its Eurasian counterpart, the common sandpiper, on the White Nile and in Galway and in the far-off mountains of New Guinea); one bright noon at the Strait of Magellan, the white-rump passed along the shore in flocks. I have seen golden plover on Alaskan tundra and in the cane fields of Hawaii, and heard the black-belly's wild call on wind-bright seacoast afternoons from Yucatán to the Great Barrier Reef.

The voice of the black-bellied plover carries far, a fluting melancholy *toor-a-lee* or *pee-ur-ee* like a sea bluebird, often heard before the bird is seen. In time of storm, it sometimes seems to be the only bird aloft, for with its wing span of two feet or more, the black-bellied plover is a strong flier; circumpolar and almost cosmopolitan, it migrates down across the world from breeding grounds within the Arctic Circle. Yet as a wanderer it is rivaled by several shorebirds, not least of all the sanderling of the Sagaponack beach, which ranks with the great skua and the Arctic tern as one of the most far-flung birds on earth.

The sanderling is the white sandpiper or "peep" of summer beaches, the tireless toy bird that runs before the surf. Because of the bold role it plays in its immense surroundings, it is the one sandpiper that most people have noticed. Yet how few notice it at all, and few of the fewer still who recognize it will ever ask themselves why it is there or where it might be going. We stand there heedless of an extraordinary accomplishment: the diminutive creature making way for us along the beaches of July may be returning from an annual spring voyage which took it from central Chile to nesting grounds in northeast Greenland, a distance of 8,000 miles. One has only to consider the life force packed tight into that puff of feathers to lay the mind wide open to the mysteries—the order of things, the why and the beginning. As we contemplate that sanderling, there by the shining sea, one question leads inevitably to another, and all questions come full circle to the questioner, paused momentarily in his own journey under the sun and sky.

But this essay will proceed objectively, laying aside the essence of the shorebird in favor of its identity—its taxonomic rank, in other words, in that order of life that man has erected like a pyramid. There at the broad base of things, the protoplasmic lowlife swarms, and there on the sharpest, highest ridge, a head taller than more hairy Hominoidea, stands man. Or so we perceive it; we are the rose on the dung heap. But "zoologists, who know that there is more difference in every way between a jellyfish, a starfish and an eel than there is between an eel and a man, often have difficulty in understanding the attitude of non-zoologists. . . ."[13] And birds are much closer to us than the eel. They are high up on the pyramid, in the class Aves of our own phylum Chordata, sharing not only our vertebrae but our warm blood and central nervous system, and not a few behavioral traits besides.

Descending systematically through phylum and class, we find the shorebirds in the order Charadriiformes, which also includes the gulls, terns and auks. The suborder Charadrii, one step down, excludes all creatures but shorebirds and their strange relatives, the jaçanas, which would otherwise be homeless; the Charadrii are the subject of this essay. The Charadrii appeared on the fossil record no later than the Eocene, and some of the species presently familiar to us were flying the silent shores of the emerging continents perhaps 50 million years before early man reared up on his hind legs. Shorebird families are so widespread—the snowy plover and at least one race of stilt are found on every continent,[23] and even the specialized jaçanas, in one species or another, are found in the tropics of both Old World and New—that their place of origin is difficult to trace. However, their close relatives, the rails and cranes, which share the shorebird's arrangement of feathers as well as its tufted oil gland and its outsize caeca, are thought[52] to have originated in the Old World.

For reasons apparent when one looks at it (the American species has a bright yellow frontal shield, in addition to elongated claws and toes, short rounded wings and wing spurs) the jaçana has not always been called a shorebird, and it is still considered a transitional form between the shorebirds and the rails. The delicate remains of birds do not survive well in the form of fossils, so that the ancestry of many species is obscure; this circumstance, together with the strictures of systematics, has kept such inconvenient species as the jaçana in a kind of limbo. Each bright new nail of information, far from strengthening the taxonomic structure, is more likely to shake and resettle the whole rickety edifice: The odd jaçana, before the century is out, may well be demoted once again to the rails and cranes, still blissfully innocent of its brief eminence among the shorebirds.

At this point, a glance at the vocabulary of taxonomy and classification might be useful. Briefly, then, the whimbrel, which must have several hundred local names around the world, is known to taxonomists of every nationality as *Numenius phaeopus* (the long-billed curlew is the *americanus* species of the same genus, while the Eskimo curlew is *N. borealis*), but the whimbrel is subdivided into geographic races or subspecies (in taxonomy the terms are interchangeable), each of which is identified by a trinomial. The European race, *N. phaeopus phaeopus,* is called the nominate race, and is so identified by the redundant name; it is nominate because it is the race which supplied the specimen named in the first systematic description of the species. *N. phaeopus hudsonicus* is the so-called Hudson Bay race (ranked until recently as a distinct species, the Hudsonian curlew), and so forth. The common snipe is another widespread bird of several races; other shorebirds may be limited to a single race.

Depending on one's taxonomist, there are between 180 and 200 species in the suborder Charadrii, representing 11 families: one-third of these species, divided among 6 families and 24 genera, occur in North America. (For the purposes of this essay, North America may be taken to mean the faunal area known as the Nearctic Region, which roughly includes the land mass north of the Tertiary Water Gap—the Tehuantepec

Gap—in southern Mexico, as well as the Bermudas and Greenland; the Nearctic has been stretched a little to include the two-striped thick-knee, which has occurred in Texas and is resident in southern Mexico and the Caribbean.)

The jaçana and the thick-knee point up the inexactitude of the terms "shorebird" (American) and "wader" (British) used to distinguish the suborder Charadrii from the so-called "marsh birds"—the herons, storks, ibises, rails and cranes. The troublesome jaçana is a bird of freshwater marshes, while the thick-knee is addicted to arid regions and does not wade; other shorebirds, such as the upland sandpiper and the mountain plover, are rarely found on shores either fresh or salt. Still, the kinship with the gulls and auks[89] (through an Old World shorebird family known as pratincoles) suggests a maritime origin for the Charadrii, and the term "shorebird" is a useful one for most species found in North America.

The two great shorebird families of our continent are the Charadriidae—the plovers and their allies—and the Scolopacidae—the sandpipers; the other four families—oystercatchers, jaçanas, stilts and avocets, and thick-knees—have only six representatives among them. Most shorebirds frequent open areas and the water's edge, and because of their food habits are comparatively scarce on steep shores like those of eastern Maine and in regions of negligible tide. Most are brown or gray above and pale to white below and have the long legs of wading birds and the short tails and sharp falcon wings of the fast fliers: they are among the few birds in the world that are swift on the ground as well as in the air. The plovers are distinguished by round dovelike heads and short bodies, bills and necks; the plover's eye is large and gentle, and most species lack a functional hind toe. Sandpiper bodies, which range in size from the 6 inches of the least sandpiper to the 24 or more of the long-billed curlew, tend to be more tapered, with longer and more slender bills, either straight or curved. Seen from a distance in mixed flocks, feeding undisturbed, the plovers are those which run and snatch, while most sandpipers walk and probe. But in North America the 15-odd plovers and 30-odd sandpipers vary widely in their habits and appearance, and for every general statement made about them here, there flies at least one blithe exception.

Because the members of these tribes are so various and striking (and because I am drawn to them and can write of "wisps of snipe" with pleasure; are there cleaner words in the English tongue than curlew, sanderling and plover?), the shorebirds are fit illustration for this essay on wild-animal evolution and behavior. And behavior will concern us more than hind toes or width of eye stripes. That a species may be determined or a kinship established on the basis of behavior is the postulate of the modern discipline of ethology ("the science of character": the term was used first by John Stuart Mill); in animals, the study of comparative behavior. Thus, the fact that the jaçana indulges in elaborate distractive displays in defense of eggs and young—a habit very pronounced among the shorebirds— may be more significant in determining its kinship than its spidery great feet, which are a weight-spreading adaptation to its lily-pad environment.

An early experiment with shorebird behavior was performed by Mark Catesby, whose *Natural History of Florida, Carolina and the Bahama Islands* (1754) was the sole New World natural history of distinction before Alexander Wilson's *American Ornithology* of 1809. Catesby provided a ruddy turnstone with stones to turn, the better to observe the feeding trait that gives the bird its name. In a time when scientific experiments were less complex than they are today, the bird was furnished systematically with stones that had nothing beneath them, whereupon "not finding under them the usual food, it died."

PECTORAL SANDPIPER

2

Listen again to a band of small shorebirds—stints, dotterels, knots and dunlins—conversing together as they run about on the level sands, or dropping bright twittering notes as they fly swiftly past: it is like the vibrating crystal chiming sounds of a handful of pebbles thrown upon and bounding and glissading musically over a wide sheet of ice.

—W. H. Hudson, Nature in Downland

IN THE OLD DAYS, in the south of France, the Eurasian woodcock was so poorly understood that it was thought to be the offspring of the polecat (*père de la bécasse*), and the American woodcock, which in colonial times was dismissed vaguely as a "snite" or "simp," remains a bird of mystery to this very day, despite the closest scrutiny of its habits. Study of captive birds has taught us little, even when, unlike Catesby's unfortunate turnstone, the prisoner is given food. That the woodcock can consume twice its own weight in earthworms in a 24-hour period—one of the few interesting things that has ever been observed about a confined specimen—is a poor and irrelevant phenomenon when compared to the bizarre activities in the natural state of "this mysterious hermit of the alders, this recluse of the boggy thickets, this wood nymph of crepuscular habits."[8]

In its guarded way of life, the woodcock is an exception among shorebirds, which are among the easiest of all birds to observe. Many species are unwary (at least when compared to most wild birds, which strongly resist the companionship of human beings), and in their season are exposed to view across the open places of the world. In spring and summer, breeding plovers may be found on beach, hill pasture, alkali flat and stony plain, and sandpipers too may be seen inland in numbers in the spring migrations, especially on the plains and prairies of the central continent. But as a family, the sandpipers are more northerly than the plovers, and most will nest in Canada or Alaska, in the wet muskegs and tundras to which their feeding habits are so well adapted.

An exception is the spotted sandpiper, which breeds almost everywhere in the United States; another is the willet, a breeding bird of both east coast and western prairie. The woodcock is ubiquitous east of the Mississippi, and the upland sandpiper, a grassland species, still nests here and there throughout a range which once extended from Texas and Virginia to southern Alaska. The marbled godwit and the long-billed curlew may also breed south of the Canadian border. Nevertheless, the great mixed flocks in which sandpipers are seen to best advantage are largely composed of northern nesters and, except in spring passage on the inland routes, are rarely observed far from the tide flats of the coasts: it is there, in spring or fall, that one must go to see these birds in their true element.

A shorebird flock is best approached at the flood tide, when the feeding flats are covered over; the flock will then be concentrated on high beach or sand bar, and its individuals, until now scattered, will usually have sought out other members of their own species. More often than not, the smaller species will gravitate toward the leeward end, leaving the large birds at the fore. All face the wind and take advantage of the flood to preen and doze.

In pictures, shorebirds are often shown sleeping with heads tucked beneath their wings, and though at first they do seem given to this carefree habit, the heads are actually laid among the back feathers; like most wild things, they are not easily taken by surprise. But the one-legged stance also portrayed is accurate enough; the smaller species so persist in it that they will often hop one-legged for considerable distances, and one afternoon at Sagaponack, a pectoral sandpiper alighted neatly without troubling to lower both its legs. One-legged shorebirds are commonly recorded, and while such individuals do occur, one must all but execute the more stubborn cases to get at the truth of the matter.

Except in wind, when the whole line looks hunched and wretched (the ruffled feathers are not a sign of misery but rather a step taken by the bird to increase its insulation against cold), there is usually a certain amount of vague activity—a "yawning," for example, in which one wing is stretched back across the outstretched leg on the same side, or a bill-scratching performed with the long toes, as if the creature was intent on putting its own eye out. One day a lesser yellowlegs scratched its bill while moving at speed over the pond, a maneuver which, in that wild second, made this attenuated bird fly like a sprung umbrella in a gale.

Some rumpled birds are bathing in the shallows, squatting and splashing and tossing water up onto their backs, and others are poking and preening with their bills, applying oil from the uropygial gland at the base of the upper tail feathers; this gland, which protects not only feathers but leg scales and bill, is especially well developed in birds such as ducks and shorebirds which frequent the vicinity of water.

Approached by observers, the shorebirds stir a little in discomfort, as if embarrassed by the intrusion; a few do their best to take no notice, replacing their heads among their back feathers. The sentinels among them—the whimbrel, black-bellied plover and greater yellowlegs are three wary species in a bird tribe noted for its trustfulness—have long since raised their heads, and now they run a little distance; unlike the others, the yellowlegs quite often moves *into* the water prior to taking flight. Avocets make nodding motions before flight, and dunlins and others may lift their wings above their backs in sign of uneasiness; whimbrels move toward the leader of the flock like a self-assembling machine. (The rock sandpiper of the north Pacific coasts has the bad habit of gathering for flight on the tops of boulders, from which the Aleuts knock the birds in numbers with well-aimed sticks.[8]) When the birds turn to face into the wind, they are set to go.

The larger birds are now engaged in head-bobbing, a trait of most shorebirds in moments of stress; the bobbing is also thought to be a preparatory motion for intended flight. The vertical head movements (the tail drops as the head rises, but the body remains stationary, producing a remarkably mechanical effort) are executed while the bird is standing still; in open surroundings, the birds are thus enabled to judge the distance of the approaching threat by obtaining a fix at different angles to the horizon.

Now the yellowlegs give cry. The greater and lesser yellowlegs are members of the group of sandpipers called tattlers (other tattlers in North America are the wandering tattler, the willet and the solitary and upland sandpipers), all of which are addicted to bobbing and nodding even when unmolested. While some tattlers are relatively silent, the lesser yellowlegs responds to the various situations and predicaments which confront it with at least 13 variants on its usual flight notes, gathering calls, chuckles, screams and yodels. Even so, it is less noisy than its larger relative: "Many a yellowlegs has been shot by an angry gunner as a reward for its exasperating loquacity."[8] (The black turnstone, a noisy sentinel of the Pacific coast, was often silenced for the same offense by hunters of the sea otter.[87])

In the old days on Long Island, the greater yellowlegs was called the "telltale tattler." The lesser yellowlegs was called the "lesser telltale," and its humble reputation as a small edition of the greater was affirmed by Alexander Wilson, who wrote of this species, "I have but little to say. It inhabits our sea-coasts and salt marshes during the summer, frequents the flats at low water, and seems particularly fond of walking among the mud."

On days of wind, the shorebird bands are restless, and abruptly the flock takes wing; most of the birds will defecate in one neat burst as they leave the ground. (Nervous evacuation is a trait of all the higher animals, including man, but in flying creatures there seems to be, if not good reason for it, at least the incidental benefit of reducing weight for a quick getaway.) They whirl off in small groups, by species rather than as indi-

viduals, according to a wariness which seems to increase with the species'
size. Immediately upon gaining altitude, the flocks burst apart in sudden
dives or other evasion tactics—the bird-of-prey defense, inappropriately
induced by man. They close again, for the wind birds are formation
flyers; whirring down across the water gleams and shining mud, they
twist and flare in a semaphore flight which turns the flock from light to
dark to light again. The bellies flash toward the sun and hold, for the
birds are flying on their side. Now they pick up other flocks from the
bars and margins, filling the air with arabesques of birds.

The wind birds alight, raising both wings vertically as soon as their
toes touch the ground, and while still running. Then they are off again,
like a quick puff of gray smoke.

The flocks flash past. They flare, dip, merge and part again, and dis-
appear over dark water; moments later, another flash of white, like a
burst of confetti against the blue. Then, out of innocence or inertial
reluctance to quit a feeding place, they return to the starting point,
hooking around upwind at the last moment and sweeping in like a gust
of petals. Chattering, they dart at one another or give ground, but in seconds the peck order is reaffirmed, and places are taken as before. The
cycle of bathing and preening, dozing and stretching starts again.
Though from a distance the flock looks tranquil, there is a constant shift
and flutter up and down the line.

The slack tide has come and gone, and the water falls away, faster
and faster. Soon the first birds move out into the shallows and com-
mence feeding. Most sandpipers seem as convivial when alighted as they
are in flight, rushing everywhere together in a body. But the plovers
among them tend to scatter upon alighting, raising their wings fastidi-
ously over their backs as if to keep them from being soiled by the
madding peep (the "stints" of Britain), as the smaller sandpipers are
known.

Certain species depart the sandbar altogether for favored feeding
grounds on mud flat or ocean beach. On days of onshore wind, many
small sea organisms will be washed up on the beach, and shorebirds ordinarily found on sheltered margins may follow the knots and sanderlings

out toward the surf. One hears them in the distance; in the hot summer stillness, the pearly whistle of the semipalmated plover stirs the heart.

Shorebirds, like rats, crows, men and other widespread and prosperous creatures, are euryphagous—partial, that is, to a variety of plant and animal food. Knots and other species that arrive in the Arctic early may live on grass seed, saxifrage buds and old crowberries of the previous summer until insects and pond organisms are released by thaw (ruddy turnstones have been observed to flip chips of still-frozen earth to get at moth larvae already active underneath), and the crowberry or curlewberry, *Empetrum nigrum*, is a favored food of southbound birds in the Maritime Provinces of Canada. For the avocet and the stilt sandpiper, plant foods may constitute as much as one-third of the normal diet. But most species, except under special circumstances, feed largely upon animal life; it is difficult to think of the least sandpiper as a carnivore, but such it is.

Some shorebirds pirate eggs of other birds. Egg predation has been charged against the bristle-thighed curlew, ruddy turnstone and golden plover in the seabird colonies of small Pacific islands—the curlew will snake an egg out from beneath an albatross as that bird lifts to shift a little and resettle—and also against the Eurasian oystercatcher in the tern colonies of Holland; a ruddy turnstone has been seen[79] to destroy the eggs of a red phalarope. Perhaps most shorebirds will at times succumb to this sort of opportunism. It has been noticed,[108] for example, that the whimbrel is included among the predatory birds which the black oystercatcher chases from the vicinity of its nest, along with eagles, ravens, crows and gulls.

Food taken from the ground may be laden with sand or mud, and many shorebirds wash their food by dropping it in water. The animal food taken by shorebirds is largely composed of small invertebrates— insects, worms, crustaceans, mollusks—but the greater yellowlegs and the red phalarope have a pronounced appetite for fish, the long-billed curlew fancies toads and the stilt sandpiper has been known to devour a frog—inadvertently perhaps, for according to the account,[8] it stood about for some time afterward, looking stunned. This species, in company with the Wilson's phalarope and the avocet, commonly swings its bill back and forth through the water, straining out its bits of food in a motion known as sidesweeping; to make this technique more effective, the bill of the stilt sandpiper has become slightly broadened at the tip. At other times, the stilt sandpiper pauses tensely with its bill deep in the sand, as if that member had been seized by some small humorist below.

The avocet is so given to the sidesweeping habit that its long bill, across millennia, has become specially adapted, curving upward in such a way that the bottom of the curve is swept back and forth across the shallow bottoms of the freshwater marshes and alkali lakes which the species prefers. This bottom-feeding habit, often performed in stagnant water and necessarily indiscriminate, has given the avocet chronic tapeworms and the rankest taste, so it is said, in all its delectable tribe. But it is a striking beast for all of that: it has a white body, white-and-black wings (like many white-winged birds—white pelicans, gulls, gannets, storks, the whooping crane—it has black wing tips, since white feathers, lacking pigment, are less resistant to wear and tear[109]), chestnut head and elegant blue legs; and its body, like the body of a duck, is laterally depressed, as if it had been stepped on. This is an adaptation to the avocet's aquatic habits; like the duck, it has waterproof dense feathers of the breast and belly. It can dive underwater and when in distress can swim all but submerged, stretching its neck out on the surface as if resigned to its own beheading. Ashore, this elaborate bird may form a crowd with its companions and circle slowly in a ring dance:

> In a submerged grove where patches of mud appeared above the water hundreds of Avocets were congregated. One little mud island that differed from the others in that it was quite round seemed to have a fascination for the birds, and they were packed together upon it in a mass which covered the island to the water's edge. As the island was about 12 feet in circumference the number of birds probably approximated 150. This mass of birds continued to revolve about from left to right, and being so crowded the movement was rather slow and their steps all marking time

in the march. The birds on the rim of the circle avoided walking off in the water and crowded in against the mass. Every moment or two birds would leave the milling body and fly to a neighboring mud island, and as many from nearby fly to take their places and join the mass.[33]

The recurved bill of the avocet and its close relative the black-necked stilt (not to be confused with the stilt sandpiper) has given its name Recurvirostridae to their exclusive family. In North America, all plover bills are modest and consistent, varying only in degree; a field mark of the Wilson's plover, for example, is its relatively heavy bill. The bills of the true sandpipers, conversely, are so various as to make it incredible that all their owners can be close relatives. Yet bird bills, in the evolutionary sense, are very "plastic"—responding readily to any changes in environment or food habit; in effect, they are compressed layers of epidermal cells, the "lips" of the reptile ancestor, more and more protruded. The shorebird bill is tubular, and as a guard against wear and tear it is usually hardest at the tip, although the turnstone bill is hard throughout. Most bills are of a piece from end to end, but in the woodcock, snipe and dowitchers, which may probe so deep into stiff mud that to open the bill is like opening scissors stuck into a tube, the tip of the upper mandible may be opened separately in order to grasp its prey. This tip, the better to detect worms, is fitted out with tactile corpuscles, analogous to the touch corpuscles in mammals.

Distinguished bills are also found on the curlews and the oystercatchers. The curlews have a decurved bill, like an avocet bill turned upside down. (Chicks of both avocet and curlews start out in life with short, straight bills.) These probes are well suited to the pursuit of fiddler crabs into their holes; the crabs are a main item of curlew diet. (The wrybilled plover of New Zealand has the outer quarter of its bill bent to the right, which apparently aids it in extracting small insect fugitives from their crannies.) Oystercatchers have long, hard knife-edged bills, used in dislodging limpets, smashing sea urchins and mussels and seizing minnows. The birds do not pry open oysters, as was once thought, nor do they slice the adductor muscle with which the oyster valves are closed;

they jab into the bivalve's gape ("catching" it napping: as Dr. Coues once pointed out, oysters are not difficult to overtake) and paralyze its nervous system with the action of the bill. Occasionally an oystercatcher is undone by its own prey, for should a large oyster clamp shut quickly on its bill, the bird may be held fast by its dour opponent until drowned by the tides.[96] American oystercatchers are most common in such regions as Cape Romain, South Carolina, with its combination of heavy tides and open flats of oyster clumps, but in the northern part of their range, where oysters are uncommon in the intertidal zone, the birds forego this favorite food entirely.

If the bills of sandpipers vary in shape and size, their feeding techniques vary even more. Almost every species has a special trick of one sort or another, a circumstance crucial to coexistence among birds which, the great part of the year, live and travel in mixed flocks and feed over common ground; were feeding habits identical, the stronger species would soon drive the others out. Sibling species of similar feeding habits are rarely found on the same breeding grounds, and their migration dates are often staggered so that the main wave of each arrives at a given place at a different time. The rich food supply of the intertidal substrate is usually adequate for both, even in times of high population densities, but there may be a simple lack of space on exposed bars, due to the fluctuation of the tides. On the Pacific coast, the least sandpiper in spring migrates earlier than its close relative the western, and where the two are found on the same mud flats, the much longer bill of the western, allowing it to feed in deeper water, may permit a limited sharing of the habitat: among the sandpipers, morphological divergence, particularly in body size and bill structure, is perhaps "a means by which ecological segregation is achieved in a habitat where spatial segregation is not possible."[88] On the North Atlantic coast, where the least migrates at about the same time as the semipalmated sandpiper—whose bill length, moreover, is near that of the least sandpiper—the smaller bird, making a virtue of necessity, "favors" grassy tide marsh.

Knots and dowitchers feed customarily in compact groups, shoulder to shoulder, while most plover, the greater yellowlegs and the upland and buff-breasted sandpipers scatter widely. Both of the yellowlegs and certain other sandpipers "snatch" their food as plovers do, rather than probe, and the greater yellowlegs shares with the avocet a technique of communal fishing: both will form a line with others of their kind to drive small fish into the shallows. In groups or alone, the fishing yellowlegs will sometimes tilt itself far forward and pitch drunkenly ahead, weaving and side-slipping as if struggling to keep its balance. The reason for this behavior is unknown, but one can guess that the swift and erratic descent of the feet would be confusing to small fish and would cause them to bunch and mill rather than flee. The surfbird and the spotted sandpiper stalk insects, while the semipalmated sandpiper takes them on the run; all three hunt with tail high and head low, apparently to obscure the outline of the head from the dim perceptions of their victims.

Plovers inspect loose sand or mud with a gull-like technique known as foot-patting, or "puddling." Similarly, the solitary sandpiper stirs freshwater bottoms with its foot—miraculously, without roiling—and snaps up the escapees; this bird is so graceful that, like its pratincole relations of the Old World, it habitually catches insects on the wing. (All shorebirds are graceful, but some are more graceful than others; the godwits, which sometimes hunch themselves like herons, lack the elegance of the other long-legged species.) The solitary sandpiper nods and bobs almost continuously, as with an ague, and teeters as relentlessly as the spotted sandpiper, though its "hinder parts are not quite as active and expressive as those of its spotted congener."[32]

The woodcock thumps its damp haunts with its feet, to lure worms upward to their doom; why thumping should hold this fatal attraction for the earthworm is not clear, but one recalls that rain will draw worms upward, and doubtless an inspired woodcock can drum like a local thunderstorm. Once the worm is contacted, it is sucked up intact, like spaghetti, and in more epicurean times these wholesome worms from the woodcock's stomach were prized as a delicacy called "trail."

Knot and sanderling, in season, follow the ocean beach in search of the sandfleas and other crustaceans exposed by the surf's retreat; their nonchalance in rough sea weather is matched by the surfbird, purple sandpiper and wandering tattler, which hunt where the seas crash on the rock coasts, and by the red and northern phalaropes, "the swimming sandpipers," which dart and flutter, magically unharmed, at the very crest of breaking waves.

The spin-and-dab technique of phalaropes, in which the floating bird spins round and round like something unwinding, is thought to stir up mosquito larvae so that they may be dabbed, often at the rate of five per second. This "pirouetting"—said to be invariably counter-clock-wise[91]—is apparently confined to still, cold waters where the larvae are inert and invisible.[101] In warm water or rough the habit is dispensed with, as it is on the ocean, where phalaropes feed on the crustacean known as brit, as well as minute fish, jellyfish and other members of the plankton community. The red phalarope sometimes feasts on parasites that it finds on the backs of whales.

Adaptive characters of these ocean swimmers—the red and northern phalaropes, neither one as large as a robin, occur in all the seven seas and spend most of the year upon the deep—include the large salt glands of true pelagic birds; dense breast and belly feathers with a layer of down, like those of ducks; flattened tarsi for swimming, like those of grebes; and lobate swimming feet. These special feet, quite different in each species, have encouraged taxonomists to place all three phalarope in separate genera. (The Wilson's phalarope, despite its structure, is a freshwater species that spends more time ashore than on the water, and its salt glands are rudimentary.) So well adapted to a floating life are phalaropes that they seem to scud before the slightest breeze, like feathered ping-pong balls.

The semipalmated sandpiper, as its cumbersome name indicates, has partly webbed feet, as do the willet, the black-necked stilt, stilt sandpiper, dowitchers and godwits; the avocet's feet are fully webbed. The jaçana's great attenuated toes enable it to stay afloat on lily pads, while the black oystercatcher, which frequents slippery wet rocks, has feet equipped with calks. The deep-wading black-necked stilt has the longest legs in proportion to its size of any bird on earth except the greater flamingo; as in most wading birds, the elongation of the leg occurs chiefly in the tarsus, and there is a corresponding elongation of the bill and neck, so that the bird may keep its plumage dry while feeding. All these adaptations to their environment improve the shorebirds' chances of maintaining their species in the remorseless competition for survival.

The great majority of the wind birds are characterized year-round by protective coloration, often so effective even on bare beach and open flat that the bird goes unseen until it moves. This camouflage is "the result of the selection of favorable mutations during thousands of years."[85] Like other small vertebrates (including many fish, frogs, snakes and songbirds, and certain rodents and small hoofed animals), they are abetted in their obscurity by countershading, which occurs, like flight, in many unrelated creatures and is therefore a striking example of the phenomenon called parallel evolution: In countershading, the outline of the creature tends to dissolve when a dark dorsal area, shading gradually to a ventral that is light, merges imperceptibly with the ground shadow when the sun is overhead. It is the violation of the countershading principle that causes unmolted golden and black-bellied plover, light above and dark below, to stand out at great distances on the pale ocean beaches of the fall.

Another concealment adaptation, often found in the same countershaded creature, is disruptive coloration. (One is tempted to say that the greater the number of streaks, stripes, spots and speckles the more effective the disruptive coloration, since all these tend to blur the outline; yet against the monotones of a mud flat, a great speckled bird would stand out like an ostrich.) The least, pectoral and white-rumped sandpipers will sometimes crouch down on their tarsi behind reed stumps or lumps of mud rather than fly, so excellent is their camouflage, and both snipe and woodcock are celebrated for "lying close"—depending on concealment, that is, until the final moment, when they burst from beneath the boot of man or nose of dog. By flattening themselves against the ground, shorebirds are able to decrease or eliminate the telltale shadow that gives them away, and this is true especially when the wings are slightly spread, forming a kind of flange which tapers all but imperceptibly into their surroundings. The thick-knee's dependence on disruptive coloration is so exaggerated that it will permit itself to be picked up from the stony ground on which it crouched; it seems convinced, despite the bad turn that events have taken, that it is nowhere to be seen.

More subtle is the camouflage of the piping plover, whose black broken collar and black streak of folded wing feathers are just enough to melt its sandy color into the high beaches it prefers. These black accents blend so deftly with scattered black bits of dried algae, drift sticks, broken clam shells and the egg cases of skates that the bird is hard to see even when running: it glides like a tiny shadow, like wind-shifted sand.

The snowy plover of white alkali flats and white coral beaches of the Gulf Coast is still paler than the piping plover, while the semipalmated plover, which favors wet beach and mud flat, is correspondingly darker, not only in general coloration but in the size and fullness of its black collar. It has been theorized[46] that their close relative the killdeer has two collars instead of one because in this much larger bird two collars are needed to form a disruptive pattern; a single collar would be conspicuous.

A different sort of plumage adaptation is the white rump of the white-rumped sandpiper, black-bellied plover, dowitchers and other shorebirds; as in animals like the white-tailed deer and cottontail rabbit, the white "flag" may communicate alarm to other members of the species and is thought to distract pursuers as its owner flashes back and forth. Perhaps the striking willet wing serves this same purpose, breaking the outline of the bird for the hawk descending from above.

Conspicuous feathering may also function as "recognition marks" for birds of the same species. While these epigamic or display markings, almost alone among bird characters, are believed to evolve quite independently of climate or environment, they may be adaptive nonetheless: The patterns of certain animals, the regularity or beauty of design, serve other members of their own species as "releasers" ("the devices for the issuing of releasing stimuli—regardless of whether the releasing factor be optical or acoustical, whether an act, a structure or a color"[51]). Also, the bright markings of many birds—and of skunks, certain insects, parrot fish and other creatures—serve notice, to pursuers, of repulsive taste, and conceivably this is true of the avocet, which is a rarity among shorebirds both in bright display characters and poor flavor. Thus the plumage of a bird may function as a "releaser" or as a means of concealment or as a means of threat and/or recognition and display: in the case of the willet, which is the drabbest of all shorebirds until like a huge butterfly it spreads its wings, the plumage may serve multiple purposes, according to need.

In the ringed plovers (genus *Charadrius*: in North America, the piping, snowy, semipalmated, Wilson's and killdeer) and in birds such as the surfbird, oystercatcher, snipe, pectoral sandpiper and others, plumages are much alike all year, probably because none of these species, even when nesting, varies much in its choice of terrain; for example, the surfbird, which deserts the Pacific seacoast for the central mountains of Alaska, seeks out a rock-heap environment in both habitats. Other species of stable appearance, like the avocet and stilt, nest in colonies where camouflage is not a factor. (On the contrary, colonial nesters are often white or otherwise brightly marked, possibly as a means of signaling across great distances the presence of food or other reason for convention.[4])

But beach species which breed inland, such as the knot and various peep, change from littoral grays and stony browns to the streaky grass buff and warm rusts that meadow birds such as the pectoral sandpiper wear all year-round. Even the bright nuptial plumage of the golden and black-bellied plovers may serve as camouflage in the dark-ploughed fields of the spring route, inland, and on the "black" tundra lichens sought by both species; in combination with their head and neck stripes, their black bellies make a disruptive pattern very difficult to pierce, though bold in coloration.

The pervasive monotones of bare terrains, encouraging cryptic markings, have made the wind birds rather subdued in plumage, and such bright color as they have is usually found in leg and bill; even the avocet, American oystercatcher and ruddy turnstone are more striking in pattern than in hue. But inevitably, a thing well suited to its surroundings—a snowflake, a sailing ship or a spoon—acquires a true beauty of refinement: the soft dove-brown of the buff-breasted sandpiper, the sun color of the golden plover, the warm leaf tones of the woodcock are essences of earth and grass, of cloud shadow and the swift seasons.

LAPWING

GOLDEN PLOVER

3

Shigi tōku
Kuwa susugu
mizu-no uneri Kana

Afar, shorebirds are flying.
Near, the water ripples,
washing the hoe.

—*Buson (Eighteenth century)*

I
N NATURE WRITINGS of more innocent days, the piping plover of the Sagaponack dunes might have been called an "angel-voiced and mist-winged breath of ocean foam," but today it is more likely to be regarded as a highly modified theodont reptile (the theodonts were small bipedal reptiles of the Triassic), related quite closely to the huge, slow cold-blooded beasts of vanished ages. (*Archaeopteryx lithographica*, the crow-sized link between the birds and reptiles, has been called by some a "specialized dinosaur"—bird feet, feathers and

all.) *Charadrius*, the genus which includes the piping plover, and *Numenius*, the genus of modern curlews, are found in the fossil records of 65 million years ago, and to this day they retain the body scales, condyle bone sockets, air sacs, nucleated red corpuscles, eggs and egg teeth in the young, which are the heritage of the reptile ancestor. Yet *Charadrius melodus* is far more changed from *Archaeopteryx* than pictures might suggest, and nowhere are the improvements better shown than in the mechanisms and adaptations necessary for long-distance flight.

Extensive flight, in fact, would be impossible without the modern sternum, which long ago supplemented the rib cage structure of *Archaeopteryx*. The sternum is a kind of breastplate with a projecting keel, familiar to all who have ever carved a bird, and the keel serves as a base for the huge wing and breast muscles which sustain strong rapid flight; these muscles form the breast meat. (Dark breast meat is the sign of a rich blood supply—the blood brings the fuel and oxygen which are burned rapidly in flight, and carries off the wastes—and it is characteristic of wild birds. Even nonmigratory grouse and quail have darker meat than domestic fowl, which, grounded for many centuries, have gone pale in wing and breast, while retaining dark meat in the legs.)

Flight muscles are extremely heavy—in some birds, they comprise half the total weight—but this weight is balanced out by lightness elsewhere. Modern birds have hollow pneumatic bones, and they have dropped the teeth of *Archaeopteryx* at one end and contracted the tail bone into a pygostyle at the other: swifts, shorebirds (the upland sandpiper is an exception), wild duck and many other strong fliers have scarcely any tail at all. Separate bones of pelvis, vertebral column and wrist and hand have become fused, and other small bones have disappeared entirely. Most skin glands are absent, and the heavy gonads atrophy to insignificance after the breeding season. A large four-chambered heart, high blood pressure and a complex respiratory system (though bird lungs are small and compact, their lung cells receive more pure fresh air than those of mammals) are other components in an exquisite mechanism pruned and pared and honed and tuned by the winds of ages.

The fuel for this machine is a rich and concentrated food used so efficiently that a strong flier like the golden plover, drawing great energy from a blood-sugar concentration nearly twice that found in mammals, may lose no more than an ounce of body weight in a flight of a thousand miles. Its economy is a condition of this plover's immense journeys: the minimum 2050-mile flight between Hawaii and the Aleutians has been computed to require 35 hours at approximately "28.5 yards, or two wingbeats, per second."[97] Lacking mammalian skin glands, the plover retains almost all the water that it takes in and eliminates, not urine, but a crystalline uric acid in the feces. Yet despite the efficiency of its machine, the obstacles which must be overcome by such a fragile organism as the wind bird remain formidable.

The swift metabolism demanded by the shorebird's rapid digestion and expenditure of energy has its disadvantages. The reptilian scales still visible in bird legs and claws are modified in the feathers to conserve warmth; bird plumage, ruffled, provides thick insulation, and there is a relative absence of bare skin and fleshy limbs. Nevertheless, a bird as small as the least sandpiper must eat frequently, for otherwise in a very few hours it would starve to death or die of cold; like all small warm-blooded creatures, it suffers from a drastic ratio between its comparatively large heat-losing surface and small heat-producing engine. (It is often said, correctly, that warm-blooded creatures smaller than hummingbirds and shrews could not feed fast enough to keep themselves alive even if they devoted all their energies to eating.) This ratio is the basis of an ecological principle known as Bergmann's rule, which states that creatures living in cold climates tend to be larger than their relatives of warm climates: the purple sandpiper, one of the largest of the genus *Calidris*,[74] is also the most northerly in year-round range, while the least sandpiper is the smallest and most southerly in the same genus. (The purple sandpiper is also the darkest-colored of its genus, supporting Gloger's rule that black pigment tends to evolve in wet climates, brown in drier ones. Also, this obliging bird has comparatively short legs, wings and bill, in seeming illustration of Allen's rule—usually applied to mammals—that creatures of cold climates, by comparison to their more southerly relatives, have smaller appendages, to reduce loss of heat. The shorebird habit of standing on one leg may derive from an instinct to keep the exposed surfaces to a minimum.)

The speed and endurance which reflect the efficiency of its machine are matched by the shorebird's maneuverability. The flock evolutions that many species make repeatedly and at high speed are so unified and intricate and marvelous that one can scarcely believe that they fly by sight or signal. The flock seems to travel as a single bird, a single soul— as if, in the intensity of flight, it had pierced a dimension of reality, of *knowing* in which all signals were superfluous.

> Everyone who has been on the shore during winter, on a day gleaming and cloudy, may have seen the masses of these birds at a distance, when the whole were only visible, appear like a dark and swiftly moving cloud, suddenly vanish, but in a second appear at some distance, glowing with a silvery light almost too intense to gaze upon, the consequences of the simultaneous motions of the flock, at once changing their position, and showing the dark gray of their back, or the pure white of their underparts.

This nineteenth-century description from Wilson's *American Ornithology* was inspired by the "ash-colored sandpiper," *Tringa canutus* (named by Linnaeus after [King] Canute, who loved to eat it, but now assigned to the genus *Calidris* and called knot) but applies as well to other shorebirds which travel habitually in flocks. Sometimes these performing flocks are mixed, but in this case the several species are of a general size and conformation, so that uniformity of flight can be maintained.

> The afternoon sun leans its rays into the repose of the marshes, when suddenly one of these tremendous floods of life surges over them, sweeping down in the distance like a cloud detached from the sky, an invasion of Valkyrie with all the wild discipline and exultation of speed and none of the menace or terror. The little birds approach over the water in a dense column of perfect order, in a humming volume of a sealike monotone, accompanied by a soft purr from thousands of throats. . . . Changing pat-

tern, direction, color and formation with every turn, each individual yet keeps the same distance from his neighbor, the same momentum and the same angle of the body, as though pulled hither and thither with lightning rapidity from the ends of an infinite number of invisible and equidistant threads, all radiating from a common point. Thus they cut one design after another out of the fabric of space—3,000 leaderless birds, executing intricate movements with the single cohesion of one body, supported upon one pair of wings. . . [32]

Such flight would not be possible without the shorebird's high-speed wings—blade wings of low camber and high aspect ratio, bearing a minimum of drag. Not all shorebirds are so swift and gifted as the knot and dunlin, nor do all of them have pointed wings, but the few exceptions, like the stilt, avocet and woodcock, make short migrations, or, like the jaçana, none at all. (This would seem to bear out Rensch's rule that "species of forms from colder climates have relatively narrower and more pointed wings in comparison with the broader, shorter wings characteristic of warmer regions."[42]) The stilt sandpiper and the two dowitchers have relatively short wings, more practical in taking flight from the deep shallows in which they feed, and possibly they are slower than their relatives, though this has to be proved: a flock of dowitchers twisting down across the Sagaponack flats looks as swift as any other.

The snipe and the pectoral sandpiper—and the least sandpiper when flushed while all alone[8]—have a wild zigzag escape flight, as all gunners know who have ever tried to shoot one. (It is probably not coincidence that the three zigzagging species are all partial to grassy mud flats, where single least sandpipers would most logically be found; yet no explanation can be offered for this parallel behavior, unless one considers it pure imitation. It might behoove the least sandpiper, that is, to imitate the evasive tactics of a fellow fugitive. Imitation in birds is so pronounced that an individual will often preen or feed simply because others are doing so and will often doze away, unfed and hungry, in the vicinity of food, if others which have eaten are dozing, also.[4]

The woodcock, of course, lacks the speed of the birds of open spaces. Its wing, like the wing of many woodland birds, is of an elliptical shape designed for navigation among tree limbs, and it has perfected a "rocketing" takeoff which carries it straight up through the branches and away, like a tiny helicopter. The spotted sandpiper and wandering tattler share a technique in which only the tips of their outstretched wings are "shivered" to maintain flight, a trait which will identify them at almost any distance. Curlews and turnstones and mountain plover may indulge in a flapping-and-sailing flight, like that of ibis; the upland sandpiper and lesser yellowlegs drift like gulls high in the blue. The long-billed curlew sometimes flies in V formation, like wild geese, and the V formation has also been noted in the golden plover and other shorebirds in migration time. It has long been assumed that the V formation gave aid and comfort to all but the leader of the flock, each bird gaining lift as well as rest by following on the slip stream of another; while this is debatable, some aerodynamic advantage is certainly involved.

The high-powered habits of migratory birds demand, if not reasoning, at least the ability to learn by trial and error and habituation. "The degree to which a given behavior pattern is modifiable by experience . . . is broadly a measure of learning or intelligence."[109] Homeothermism, or warm-bloodedness, which permits bird activity all year-round, even in cold climates, "makes possible a continuity of experience that powerfully supports the learning process."[109]

A simple example of trial-and-error learning, cited earlier, might be the consumption by the stilt sandpiper of a frog too large for it; the sandpiper learned that its eyes were bigger than its gullet. Habituation, on the other hand, is based on an acquired tolerance of local conditions: killdeer soon learn to remain calm in the proximity of gunfire, provided that the gunfire is not directed at themselves, and may lay and defend a clutch of eggs in a busy driveway, returning to the nest after cars have passed over it.[1] There is no example among shorebirds of "insight learning"—that apprehension of relationships that permits certain birds to use tools (Galapagos woodpecker finch, Indian tailorbird), to count (crows: up to three) or to operate devices of man's construction that reward their ingenuity with food (titmice).

Whether one takes the mechanistic view that birds are simply reflex organisms whose every act, no matter how elaborate, can be accounted for in terms of instinct, or the vitalist view that in addition to their instincts birds often act on individual initiative—the truth is almost certainly somewhere between—one must concede that they are unintelligent. Ironically, the power of flight, which we regard as the bird's most magnificent attainment, has also been the evolutionary adaptation which has held it well behind the mammals in intelligence. "In effect, flight has become a substitute for cleverness; birds solve many potential problems merely by flying away from them."[109] Yet quick and positive reactions are demanded of the wind bird, or of any bird that moves at high speeds, migrates great distances against great obstacles, hunts food and escapes enemies. Many such problems, solved by mammals with conscious movement, are referred by the shorebird to a complex central nervous system which in part replaces true intelligence.

In addition to dullness of mind, birds seem blunted in almost all the sensory perceptions. Their powers of touch and smell are rudimentary (though kiwis, chickens, certain pelagic birds and at least one species of vulture have been shown to possess a sense of smell, and doubtless there are others), and for most birds, the ear serves chiefly as an organ of equilibrium, despite the important role of calls and birdsong. But some shorebirds have ear openings of different sizes on each side of the head, an arrangement—noted especially in owls—which apparently serves to fix the location of important sounds.

Deficiencies in the other senses are more than offset by the excellence of bird vision: The small bird head seems little more than a kind of eye case, in which the convex surfaces of the eye sockets may even touch. Shorebird eyes have high resolving power and color vision, and some are equipped with twin fovea—small rodless areas in each retina which afford a sharp wide view of the surroundings. The eyes of the woodcock, a bird of crepuscular habits, are relatively large, like those of owls; the thick-knee is also crepuscular, and the eyes of both birds, after dark, reflect light with an eerie glow, as red as coals.

Most shorebird eyes are laterally placed, enabling them to see equally well up, down and in all directions. (The owls, which do not have to concern themselves about attack, have eyes facing directly forward, while the down-directed eyes of the bittern face forward only when it stands, as it is wont to do, with its bill pointed at the sky.) The eyes of the woodcock, however, crowd upward toward its crown and are set slightly to the rear, the better to detect foul play which might come at it from above and from behind; as a result, its cerebral axis is so far tipped back that its brain is almost upside down.[16] That it actually sees better backward than forward may or may not account for the tendency of this peculiar bird to collide with tree limbs.

SNOWY PLOVER

BLACK-NECKED STILT

4

Did you ever chance to hear the midnight flight of birds passing through the air and darkness overhead, in countless armies, changing their early or late summer habitat? It is something not to be forgotten. . . . You could hear . . . "the rush of mighty wings," but oftener a velvety rustle, long drawn out . . . occasionally from high in the air came the notes of the plover.

—*Walt Whitman,* Specimen Days

THE WIND BIRDS are strong, marvelous fliers, averaging greater distances in their migrations than any other bird family on earth. Of the several hundred migratory birds of North America, only 35 winter as far south as central Chile, and in this group the barn swallow, blackpoll warbler and Swainson's thrush, the osprey, broad-winged hawk and peregrine, with a few gulls, fly that far only irregularly. All the rest of the 35 are shorebirds, several of which go all the way to land's end, near Cape Horn.[21] The white-rumped sandpiper, which flies 9,000 miles twice every year in pursuit of summer, is only exceeded in the distance of its north-south migration by the Arctic tern, and the golden plover far exceeds the tern in the distances covered in a single flight; it is thought to travel well over 2,000 miles nonstop on both its Atlantic and Pacific migrations. The bristle-thighed curlew, which flies from Alaska to Polynesia and New Zealand, is another distance flier of renown; and so are the ruddy turnstone, wandering tattler and sanderling, which may be found on the most far-flung strands and atolls throughout their enormous range.

Because of the great distances they must travel, the migrants make preparations to depart again within a few months of their arrival from the north; the flocking and reflocking that is evident on the summer coasts and pampas of the Southern Hemisphere is a symptom of premigratory restlessness. This restlessness is not entirely attributable to activity of the glands, for castrated birds will migrate,[109] borne along, perhaps, by the northward tide of movement. Migration is part of an annual cycle which also includes breeding and molt; what is not yet fully known is the exact pattern of stimuli, physiological and/or external, that puts this cycle into motion.

Temperature, which was long assumed to be the controlling factor, is now thought to have no effect at all, but it is generally agreed that the onset of warm weather, with an increased food supply and a lessened heat loss, gives the bird the excess energy which is expressed in migration and reproduction. Food supply, light intensity, seasonal rains and many other forces, including internal rhythms of the glands, may help incite the reproductive dance, but the strongest goad of all appears to be reaction to a change in light as the season turns; this reaction, in both plants and animals, is called photoperiodism. The intensity of illumination, however, is probably less important than the longer day in which to remain active. "Daylight probably stimulates gonads not because it is beneficial to general well-being, but because a physiological timing mechanism has been evolved between gonad development and an external factor associated with spring."[48] Thus, birds which winter in the West Indies or the southern states are thought to be stirred in early spring by the lengthening of the days.

But the spotted sandpiper may fly to the region of the equator, where day length is constant throughout the year; and where the white-rumped sandpiper winters in the uttermost part of the earth, the summer days of February, far from lengthening, grow shorter with the advent of the Capricornian autumn. Unless they possess some internal chronometer quite independent of external stimuli, the equatorial migrants must be awakened from the sameness of their days by some such phenomenon as a change in the rains or the northerly drift of the sun, while the species wintering in austral latitudes may be stirred by the *shortening* of days toward such activities as song, mock fighting and formation of pairs which are the external symptoms of pituitary change.

By February, in Tierra del Fuego, male white-rumped sandpipers are already engaged in mock battles with other males of their own kind. The birds circle like midget roosters, leaping up and down with sexual rage, but never touching. Their mock fights are not a sign of distaste for their own kind but of an impulse to perpetuate it; the time of premigration courtship has begun. On the northern continent, a few woodcock have already begun to nest; the snipe and killdeer, in late February, would be winging northward, crowding the retreat of frozen earth.

Within the body of the sandpiper strange stirrings are taking place. Its gonads quicken and enlarge, though not so grossly as to slow its flight in the great journey to come. Fully developed gonads have little or no effect on the migratory impulse, though the impulse is stimulated by partial development of these glands. Deposits of fat—the fuel for the journey—begin to form beneath the skin. The amount of fat is dictated by the rigors of the bird's migration. The Eskimo curlew made long transoceanic flights and its thin skin was stretched so taut with stored-up fat that in the days when it was shot by thousands from the sky, the fat would sometimes burst out of its breast when it struck the ground. In New England, for this reason, it was called the dough-bird.

The gland quickening and fat accumulation which encourage the white-rump's hypertonic belligerence also produce a symptom known as *Zugunruhe*, or migration restlessness, which is confined to migratory birds; many shorebirds travel through the night, and a wild bird held captive in its time of passage will sleep for a short time after sunset, then become more and more fretful until nearly midnight, when the fever of flight begins to taper off. *Zugunruhe*, which is inhibited in spring by a turn of cold weather and in autumn by a spell of warmth, is ordinarily accompanied by compass orientation: if placed outdoors where it can see the stars, the captive will face north in spring and southward in the fall.

The urge to migrate is strongest in birds of the cold climes of the northern continent, where seasonal changes in climate are most pronounced; a few austral species migrate *south* to breed, returning northward to escape Antarctic winter (the lesser seed snipe nests in Tierra del Fuego and winters in central Argentina, while the Magellanic snipe winters north to Uruguay), but the migrations are much shorter, for the range in temperature is less.

Migration routes apply more rigidly to species than to the individual shorebird, which may adjust its heading and even its route and destination from year to year, depending on whim and circumstance. But the piping plover, ruddy turnstone and sanderling have been known to return to the same nesting ground, in what is known as *Ortstreue* or "place faithfulness," and spotted sandpipers—presumably the same pair—have occupied the identical nest site in consecutive years.[47] A stilt sandpiper banded at Hudson Bay also returned the next year to the same scrape, and possibly *Ortstreue* occurs in shorebirds generally.

As the time to migrate nears, the shorebirds rise and form huge flocks and veer apart in small ones, accumulating in the air again like bits of mercury, alighting for a quick moment before breaking away anew. They are frantic to be off, yet the last impulse has not come that will whirl them from the shore and send them spinning to the altitudes, perhaps three miles in the air, that are best suited to the spanning of the earth.

A meteorological signal may release them. Electricity in the air affects the migration behavior of curlews, oystercatchers and others,[27] though these effects are not well understood. And unlike birds of fixed migration dates, such as certain swifts and swallows, shorebirds may be delayed a month or more by high-pressure areas to the north. This indicates that the migration impulse, however strong, is not likely to run away with the bird in the face of adverse conditions.

On the other hand, bad weather encourages the flock instinct in birds by inhibiting spring sexuality and belligerence: "the factors which are associated with increased flocking are those that may be considered unfavorable.[30] Cold or famine or the dangers of migration tend to draw the birds together: as social creatures, they need one another, and in hard times the need triumphs over the seasonal intolerance brought on by awakening hormones. Therefore, the wind birds are flocked and ready to be off when the first pale band of light breaks the horizon.

Most birds of open spaces are gregarious by nature, as if otherwise, in the vastness of a world where all horizons are so distant, they would be little more than windblown scraps. The flock, with its cumulative sense of direction, serves as protection for individuals against straying off into infinities; a tired bird can benefit from the experience of the leaders. It is also a defense against the predators; hawks seem daunted by the unity or just plain bulk of a close flock. (This phenomenon has been well described in regard to schools of fish—the "mystical sort of protective anonymity, thought to confound a predator unable to concentrate its hunger on any one of such a host."[14]) Most shorebirds, like ducks and other birds, cluster together in time of peril, and white-rumped sandpipers may rush at a predator in a body and scatter in its face in a "confusion" attack which usually turns it aside.

The ruddy turnstone, though it migrates in small groups, "is not particularly sociable. . . . I have occasionally observed a marked hierarchy in a party of only two birds, the inferior individual avoiding the superior one."[91] And the Wilson's plover, in company with the snipe and woodcock, the spotted sandpiper and most of the tattlers (the lesser yellowlegs is an exception), is a casual flocker at best. The solitary sandpiper, even if apprehended in a group, will scatter when it takes flight—entirely unlike the great majority of sandpipers, whose habit of snapping together in the air like magnets was of no small convenience to the gunner in the days when they were shot. Some nonflockers have either a short migration span or inland habitats where flocking would be a nuisance, but the greater yellowlegs may keep its own company all the way from Tierra del Fuego to Alaska.

Then the flocks are gone. On tide flats which at twilight of the evening past had swarmed with shorebirds, dirtied feathers drift across white-spotted mud, and hard shreds of dried algae, and brown spindrift, and the husks of dead crustaceans. The solitary birds that pass look forlorn and indecisive, and in the emptiness their calls receive no answer; these are the sick, weak, injured and immature, whose impulses were not strong enough to hurl them upward at the northern stars. Now, they must wait out the southern winter. Greater and lesser yellowlegs are common birds in the Argentine throughout the year, and the Hudsonian godwit was once so widespread on the pampas from April to September that naturalists of 80 years ago called them a population of "Antarctic" breeders.

Most of these nonmigrants are yearling birds. Even in species that are sexually mature in their second year, not all individuals go north to breed; in the surfbird, for one, it appears doubtful that yearlings visit the breeding range at all.[74] And the mature birds make no attempt to breed on winter grounds: there is no nesting record on its winter range for a migratory species from North America. (The jaçana, killdeer, Wilson's plover, American oystercatcher and black-necked stilt that nest in South America are resident there, and it is conceivable that other species will one day join them; in the Old World, *Tringa hypoleucos*, the common sandpiper, has established a nesting population in its former winter quarters in South Africa.[27])

The black-necked stilt and the jaçana are all-year residents throughout most of their range, and several other shorebirds—the willet, avocet, oystercatchers and Wilson's plover—"migrate" largely in a local sense, according to regional weather and conditions, or may even forego migration entirely. The fact that certain populations of the migratory killdeer, snowy plover and rock sandpiper have become nonmigratory where conditions suit them suggests that migration is not innate behavior, but rather an evolutionary response to external pressures; the glaciers of the Pleistocene, which forced huge populations southward and encouraged a northward surge as they withdrew, must have affected the migration patterns of nearly all shorebirds of the northern continent.

By early March, the flocks have left Tierra del Fuego and Patagonia;

moving north, they join those relatives that wintered on the pampas, or along the tropical rivers and savannas, or on white coral shores of the Caribbean. On the moonlike desert beaches of Peru, shrouded by fogs drifted in off the Humboldt Current, the black-bellied plover runs and watches, runs and watches; already the plumage of its silver breast has taken on a fretting of the bold black that it will carry north to the Arctic.

Left behind on ocean coasts from Panama to California and New England are those individuals whose energies got them underway but did not drive them to complete their journey. These birds—the ones seen in the northern states on the beaches of late June—may have set out with their fellows out of pure sociability, for birds, like dogs and men, are drawn to movement. On June 26, 1964, there was a flock of thirty-odd black-bellied plover on the ocean beach a few miles from Sagaponack; despite the surprising number, one must assume that all these were nonbreeders, for this plover nests within the Arctic Circle.

Because of the pressures of the breeding cycle, spring migration is performed much more rapidly than migration in the fall. Northbound dunlin, passing a light plane, have been timed at 110 miles per hour,[62] or nearly twice the usual recorded flight speeds of other shorebirds. Birds, when pressed, are capable of a sharp increase in velocity, and in the thin air of high altitudes, migrants probably travel at a rate rarely attained nearer the ground. The bristle-thighed curlew flies the 6,000 miles or more from New Zealand to its nesting grounds in western Alaska in about six weeks, while the southward journey may take twice as long. Birds winging northward from the Argentine move with corresponding haste. There appear to be few feeding grounds on the muddy coasts of northern South America and in the almost tideless Caribbean, and the golden plover may sometimes fly from the beaches of Peru all the way to the Gulf Coast without alighting.[21] (The bladder snail *Physa* has been found in both crop and plumage of certain migrant plover, encouraging the startling idea that these birds might deliberately place snails in their plumage before starting on a long voyage in order to provide themselves with at least one meal during the trip.[90])

By late March and early April, when the wind birds appear in the big

skies of the Gulf of Mexico, the killdeer, snipe and woodcock that wintered on the Gulf Coast may already have flown to southern Canada:
The woodcock nests so very early—there are records for December in
Louisiana, January in Texas and February in North Carolina—that
sometimes bird and nest together are covered up by snow, and its young
may be close to flight by the time other wind birds arrive in the Arctic. A
few woodcock, in favorable years, have remained as far north as Long
Island, and where warm springs or other special conditions permit, the
common snipe will winter north beyond the line of frozen ground; it has
been found in Nova Scotia bogs in the dead of winter, with the glass
near zero. In mid-February of 1965, after a hard January, a lone snipe
could be seen each day in a winding cattail "dreen" on the east side of
Sagaponack Pond, probing the mud (which proved to be full of tiny
worms) along the very edges of the ice cakes.

Shorebirds, being highly mobile, will fly before storm or unseason-
able turn of weather, but sometimes they are caught off guard by sudden
freezes. On February 13 of 1899, northbound woodcock, driven back
toward the south, appeared near Charleston in the tens of thousands.
They were half-starved and bewildered and were killed or died. Yet
species of less specialized food habits can endure very low temperatures;
at Sagaponack, the sanderlings and greater yellowlegs, which are present
until mid-January, will sometimes overwinter, and are usually quite common in March—though Sagaponack in the spring is a lean feeding
ground for shorebirds, and even the semipalmated sandpipers, so abundant in summer and fall, mostly forsake the cold Atlantic beaches for an
inland journey up the Mississippi Valley.

On the last day of April, a few years ago, there came from the sea a
mixed flock of red and northern phalarope, some 60 birds in all. They
rode out the two days of an easterly gale on a small pond connected to
Sagaponack Pond by the small stream where I saw the winter snipe. Two
red phalarope were in full nuptial plumage, bright chestnut and gold,
and they led the small band which bobbed on the gray wavelets or
ruffled its feathers in the salt grass, awaiting a shifting of the skies that
would draw the wind birds onward to the Arctic.

DOTTEREL

KILLDEER

5

. . . None should dare to be out of doors;
Remain in your retreats or emigrate,
Following the wild duck's or snipe's or crane's course.
You are handicapped by fate,
And cannot skim waves, then skirt leagues of sand
In searching out some other land.

     —La Fontaine, Fables *(translated by Marianne Moore)*

B Y MAY the great migration routes have opened out, scattering shorebirds all across the north. The hardy black turnstone, migrating across the water from California, is one of the first shorebirds to appear on the coast of west Alaska, and the ruddy turnstone, knot and sanderling fly much farther still, nesting as close to the North Pole as farthest Ellesmere Island, near latitude 83. These species breed discontinuously all around the Arctic circumference, and so close to the North Pole that a sanderling in Russia and another in Canada may nest no more than 1,000 miles apart over the top of the world. Other shorebirds are not far to the south, including the Baird's sandpiper, which also nests entirely within the Arctic Circle, under the midnight sun.

It would seem logical that a species hardy enough to winter in North

America would nest correspondingly farther north than relatives that come from South America, but except for the dunlin and a few others, the exact reverse is true. Even the purple sandpiper, uncommon in winter south of New Jersey, flies no deeper into the Arctic than do several species that winter in South America. Many species which winter in the United States migrate northward little if at all, and others move but a limited distance into southern Canada.

In other words, a strong migratory urge impels the bird to great lengths in *both* directions; this phenomenon, called leap-frog migration, in which northerly breeders also winter farther south than more sedentary relatives of the same or related species, is very pronounced among the shorebirds.

The species breeding south of Canada are very much in the minority. Most of the world's sandpipers breed in the far north, which has led to the supposition that the Scolopacidae, at least, originated in the Northern Hemisphere; shorebirds make up two-thirds of the few nesting species that are not common to the Arctic bird fauna of both Asia and America.[58] Twenty-three North American shorebird species nest customarily beyond the Arctic Circle; thirteen more nest north of the Canadian border; and another thirteen breed in Canada as well as the United States, leaving but seven species of shorebirds—jaçana; thick-knee; American oystercatcher; snowy, mountain and Wilson's plovers; and black-necked stilt—that confine their breeding on this continent to the United States. In Audubon's time, the American oystercatcher bred in Labrador, and one day it may do so again.

Paradoxically, this southern group includes none of the most familiar species; it is the woodcock and the common snipe, which are still included among the game birds, that are the best-known shorebirds in America. The snipe is also known through euphemisms: "snipe hunt" and "gutter snipe" are familiar terms, and the word "sniper" was doubtless used first to describe a man skilled enough with a gun to hit such erratic fliers. (Even in the old days, the snipe was a favorite among sportsmen; it was not only abundant and widespread but owing to its hardihood was an available target the greater part of the year, being common throughout the winter in the southern states. Careful records kept from 1867 to 1887 by James J. Pringle, a southern gentleman of Louisiana, indicate a personal bag of 69,087 snipe, plus several thousand other birds "killed incidentally."[8] Since many gunners consider the snipe the most difficult of all gamebirds to bring down, these figures bear stern witness to Mr. Pringle's prowess as well as to snipe prosperity: Pringle notes one splendid day when over the space of six hours the snipe fell to his gun at better than one a minute. To achieve his records, Mr. Pringle employed two beaters, a marker and one or two retrievers, though "I shot with only one gun at a time; had no loader, but loaded my gun myself.")

The snipe is a quite common bird even today, but the average person, lacking a taste for marshy ground and "snipe bogs," does not often see one. The shorebirds actually *seen* most often are probably the killdeer and spotted sandpiper, not only because they are common, but because, in more seasons than not, they may be found almost everywhere throughout the land. Unlike the woodcock, which eats earthworms almost exclusively, or the jaçana, with its specialized lily-pad habitat, both killdeer and spotted sandpiper can and will make do with a wide variety of foods, climates, local conditions and companions. This tolerance is based on a capacity for dispersal over a wide range of habitats that is the key to general distribution.

The killdeer, alone among North American ring plovers, has a shrill and strident cry, *kill-dee, kill-dee,* that has earned it both its common name and the species name *vociferus.* Its voice, which may be heard day or night, is a familiar one to the majority of rural inhabitants of the Americas, since the killdeer nests in a variety of localities from southern Canada to northern Chile. This range is matched only by the American oystercatcher which, nesting on both coasts of the United States, south into Chile and the Argentine, has the longest latitudinal breeding range of any shorebird in the Americas.

The killdeer's flexibility accounts for its irregular migration pattern; it migrates, that is, as conditions warrant, and where life suits it all year-round, it does not migrate at all. From the northern part of its range, it flies southward far enough to escape the snow, returning in spring almost as early as the red-winged blackbird. It is willing to nest on rooftops or next to the railroad tracks of man, and is partial to cleared and cultivated ground; in communities where it is common, "it is difficult to get beyond reach of its notes."[15]

Similarly, the spotted sandpiper has a vast breeding range, extending from northwest Alaska to Texas and North Carolina, and will make its home with equal aplomb at sea level or at 14,000 feet. This jaunty bird sets forth into the world straight from the egg, and if pursued, even at the tender age of several hours, will step smartly to the water and swim away. The adult swims as readily as a phalarope, and dives readily, as the phalarope cannot; in shallow water, if it pleases, "it can go to the bottom and run a short distance with head held low and tail raised like a Dipper,"[33] before its buoyancy restores it to the surface. (True underwater locomotion is uncommon among shorebirds, but almost all of them will dive and "swim" if wounded or pursued; a marbled godwit has been seen[8] to dive to escape a peregrine falcon, and snipe and other species will cling to the bottom with their bills, like wounded ducks. The jaçana, ever an exception, clings to the bottom with its feet.)

The dipper, like the spotted sandpiper, also feeds along water margins *and also teeters*, so do the water thrushes and the wagtails. (The wagtails frequent dry places as well.) The similarity of habit and habitat in species so unrelated is a striking example of parallel evolution, and surely the purpose of the teeter is common to all: The most interesting hypothesis yet put forward is that the teetering or "tipping" causes the hunting or hiding bird to "blend into the lapping wavelets and the play of light and shadow they create on shore."[40]

Among the many attainments of the spotted sandpiper is its ability to fly straight up out of the water, or for that matter, fly straight *into* it if pursued while aloft, using its wings to continue its flight beneath the surface. It seems inevitable that such a dynamic and successful bird should have an air-bubble adaptation which not only keeps its feathers dry but gives it an attractive sparkle as it promenades over the bottom.

The spotted sandpiper and the killdeer are not alone in their flexible behavior. The ruddy turnstone, turning its stone, exploits a food source not used by other shorebirds; in fact, a 15-day-old captive chick refused to feed until its food was placed under a tin water dish, which it had been overturning from the start. Thereafter, it had thrived on "moistened lune flesh,"[79] minced to caterpillar size. Yet, the adult is by no means specialized: it eats grasshoppers with relish, rifles eggs of other birds and competes truculently with larger species for eggs of the king crab. It follows the surf and tosses seaweed and sometimes, in the intensity of its pursuit of subterraneans, digs holes in the beach into which it disappears from view. In the far north it has been apprehended gorging on maggots in dead seal bodies and climbing about in bushes after berries. Not surprisingly, this aggressive and opportunistic little bird is virtually circumpolar in its breeding range, and winters in Africa, Australia and Oceania as well as South America.

Other adaptable species of wide distribution are the willet, both yellowlegs and the common snipe. The willet's breeding range, though fragmented by man, includes western prairie and alkali flat, besides a variety of coastal habitats on the Atlantic and Gulf coasts, from Texas to New Jersey, and in Nova Scotia; its diet extends from crabs to insects. The yellowlegs species, which breeds across the northern continent, from Alaska to eastern Canada, are also elastic in their diet, while the snipe finds matters to its liking almost everywhere in the Northern Hemisphere.

Pronounced tolerance and capacity for dispersal in a particular species are ordinarily accompanied by extension of its range, just as increased specialization or species senility is usually a prelude to withdrawal. Both killdeer and spotted sandpiper may be widening their range, thanks to their tolerance of man. The force, in other words, that foreshortened the ranges of the American oystercatcher, long-billed curlew and willet (and almost extinguished the Eskimo curlew and the upland and buff-breasted sandpipers) has proved a blessing to these less toothsome, less demanding species. With every new slough and farm pond, the spotted sandpiper will prosper, and the killdeer has made itself at home on airstrips and golf courses up and down the land.

Even the buff-breasted and upland sandpipers may have profited at first from the coming of the white man, who expanded their open country range by clearing primeval forest. Both nested widely on the plains and, together with the great migrating clouds of plover, curlew and other shorebirds, performed excellent service for the farmer in the destruction of grasshoppers, cutworms, wireworms and the like. Yet their role as a scourge of insects was so little appreciated that western farmers in the 1800s set out poison for them in the belief that they ate grain (among shorebirds which occur in North America, only the eccentric ruff is an habitual grain eater[8]), while sportsmen organized "spring shoots in the upper Mississippi Valley, where a wagon load of plover and curlew, heaped higher than the sideboards, was considered a fair bag. . . . If blazing away into the flocks filled the wagons up too soon, the bleeding pile was speedily dumped onto the prairie, there to rot, and the wagon loaded up all over again."[57]

Though these heroic days are gone, the prairie nesters will not recover, for much of their former grassland habitat of slough and pothole has been drained and cultivated to increase the national surplus in wheat, and the insects that they once helped control are assaulted instead by man's lunatic biocides, which have made rare birds of many species that only a decade ago were common.

The ruddy turnstone, black-bellied plover, sanderling, common snipe, whimbrel and the red and northern phalaropes are considered cosmopolitan species—they occur, that is, on nearly every continent or on all the seven seas. The Atlantic coast of the Americas excepted, the snowy (or Kentish) plover appears on almost all coasts of the world south of 50 degrees north latitude, and in various inland regions in between. The wind birds in general are so wide-ranging and mobile that even the mountains and oceans which serve as barriers to many other birds have not impeded their dispersal. And they are comparatively undisturbed by such hazards as climatic change (which affects the soil and vegetation of inland habitats more than it does the ecology of the tide line), unfamiliar foods, new predators and competition from indigenous species—any one of which is more than enough to discourage the errant land bird. Considering the strong flight of shorebirds, and the millions of years that they have had in which to spread, it seems astonishing that the world-wide species are so few, and all the more so when it is recalled that many whales and sharks, freshwater organisms, crustaceans and other creatures much less mobile are as cosmopolitan as sanderlings. More astonishing still, the Eskimo and bristle-thighed curlews, the white-rumped, buff-breasted and stilt sandpipers, the Wilson's phalarope and the surfbird breed only in North America, and the genera which include all of these birds except the white-rump and the curlews are entirely confined, in breeding time, to this continent.

Shorebird mobility is oddly demonstrated by the rock sandpiper of the Bering Sea, which is almost nonmigratory throughout its range; it winters commonly as far north as the Aleutians, with a few birds straying south along the cold Pacific coast as far as Humboldt Bay, in northern California. But a wintering population of rock sandpipers also occurs on a subtropical coast of Mexico, near Punta Piedras Blancas, in Baja California.[44] Upwelling currents of cold ocean water in this region explain its attraction for the bird; what is surprising is that this more or less sedentary sandpiper should have discovered a suitable habitat separated from its normal range by an ecological barrier of temperate water 800 miles across.

While most shorebirds are well distributed across the great shaggy head and shoulders of our continent, a few are curiously restricted in their range. The surfbird, so far as is known, nests only in the mountains of central Alaska (its winter range, on the other hand, extends from southern Alaska to the Strait of Magellan), while the Hudsonian godwit is confined to scattered localities in Alaska, the Northwest Territories and northern Manitoba. Like the Eskimo curlew and golden plover, this handsome white-rumped species undertakes long and hazardous migrations across continents and oceans—it has been suggested[39] that this species flies 3,000 miles, from James Bay to the mouth of the Orinoco, without a stop—and it was formerly exposed to man's predation, from the North Atlantic states to the pampas, and from the pampas to the

Great Plains. Audubon, who never saw it, called it "of rare occurrence in any part of the United States," but more recently, the species has been declared "a common breeding bird within a somewhat specialized but not unduly restricted range in central and northwestern subarctic Canada."[39] We can guess that its scattered nesting grounds are the remnants of a range that was much broader, and that this range had shrunk before the coming of the white men. But if so, why? It is an exceptionally unassertive bird, readily chivvied by marbled godwits and even sanderlings; was it always so timid, or is this a degeneration brought about by mutation? Has it become specialized in some way not yet understood? Was it declining long ago or was there introduced in some recent millennium a small new factor of climate or circumstance—the coming of the red man from Siberia, for example—which upset the balance to its detriment? A naturalist who could find answers to such questions would explain much that we do not know about ecology, ethology and genetics.

Another bird of limited breeding range is the western sandpiper, which nests on the Chukchi Peninsula of Siberia and on the coast of northwest Alaska east to Point Barrow and Camden Bay. At Point Barrow, its range is overlapped by that of the semipalmated sandpiper, and the two species are so similar that, did they not remain aloof from each other on the breeding grounds, they might be considered two races of a single species. Yet the semipalmated sandpiper enjoys an enormous range both latitudinally and longitudinally, singing and preening from Point Barrow on the Beaufort Sea south and east to Hudson Bay and Quebec.

What is interesting here is not the relatively restricted breeding range of the western sandpiper but the reason for it, in juxtaposition with the vast realm of the semipalmated. And we are scarcely assisted by the knowledge that, in winter, the western sandpiper is more widely distributed than its sibling species, being found on occasion from southern Alaska and New Jersey all the way down both coasts to the Gulf states, the Caribbean and South America.

The western and semipalmated sandpipers are assumed to be distinct, since their breeding ranges overlap and no hybrids have been recorded, yet how were they separated in the first place? For we can assume that at one time these two very similar little birds were one. And if—as is presently thought[61]—at least partial geographic separation of two populations of a single species is necessary in order that a new species evolve out of the old, then at one time the two were separated, and only recently, comparatively speaking, have met again on a shared breeding ground.

The overlapping ranges of these sandpipers, most notably at Point Barrow and on winter grounds in South Carolina, raises the question of Gause's principle, which states that any given ecological niche can support only a single species: where two species of common origin and habits share the same feeding ground and the same food preference, one must sooner or later change its preference or make way for the other. In the case of the shorebirds, Gause's principle seems chiefly applicable to the breeding grounds; the rich food supply so manifest on the Carolina tidal flats shared by these birds would doubtless support both species, even were their preferences identical, or nearly so. (Paradoxically, the birds may be forced to tolerate other species on migration, where shorelines are limited, in a way that they would not on the tundra, where shorelines are almost limitless.) But as a general rule—in gulls, ducks and other creatures, as well as shorebirds—"closely allied members of the same genus usually have more or less separate winter quarters on account of competition for food, some species being residents, some moving a distance to the south, others going to the tropics or even farther."[91]

In theory, the genetic changes undergone by one or both siblings during the period of separation have made them mutually infertile, or otherwise isolated in their breeding habits. And there are subtle differences of behavior: the western sandpiper tends to feed in deeper water when the two are together in mixed flocks, and the bill of a typical western is noticeably longer. Supposing (without real evidence) that the two phenomena are linked, how did this distinction come about? The western is, by all accounts, a very gentle bird, even in time of courtship; was the longer bill developed through the necessity of feeding in deeper water through inability to compete with its more aggressive relative?

This proposition, which cannot be proved, is no more outlandish than the true explanation would appear to us, were it proposed here without evidence. It is the attempt to resolve such questions that makes ethology the engrossing study that it is, and once in a while, these questions find their answer—more often than not, an answer most remarkable for its simplicity.

The shorebirds' swift wings and wide-ranging habits have spared them the fatal pattern of isolation, overspecialization and unequal struggle with new competitors which plunges most doomed creatures into extinction. Island birds, which include only 20 percent of the world's species, account for more than 90 percent of the modern forms that have disappeared. Though the Eskimo curlew, New Zealand shore plover and Jerdon's courser ("It appears to have a very limited range, having only been found in that part of the Indian peninsula which lies between 100 miles and 300 miles due north of Madras, and, curiously enough, only in open forest country"[94]) are all on the point of extinction, the one shorebird which has certainly vanished in historic times is the *te-te*, or Tahitian sandpiper. Presumably this species was sedentary and uncommon, for it is known only from three specimens collected in the Society Islands by naturalists accompanying Captain Cook. One September in Tahiti and Moorea, like many a shorebird fancier before me, I kept a wistful eye out for the *te-te*, a pretty, raillike, burnt-sienna-colored bird said to have haunted the shadowed brooks which flow down the dark volcanic mountains to the sea.

TURNSTONES

SANDERLINGS

6

. . . this ancient land . . . where wone to wail whimbrel to peewee o'er the saltings. . . .

—*James Joyce*, Finnegans Wake

I N THE MYSTERY of the western and semipalmated sandpipers, we have touched somewhat uneasily on questions of speciation and geographic races, which are chiefly interesting to the degree that they illuminate the origins, natural history and ecology of species. Subspecies that are valid are all potential species, and the characters that distinguish them from one another are not haphazard: these characters, when not in themselves adaptations to differing environments, are always symptoms of some other characters that are. Even the "bristles"— actually, barbless feather shafts—of the bristle-thighed curlew, which would seem to be the most useless of all shorebird appurtenances, may be nonadaptive visible evidence of an adaptive gene.

But in their attempts to bring order out of the chaos of relationships—a three-dimensional chaos due to the factors of extinct species
and past time—taxonomists have enmeshed themselves in debatable
anatomical peculiarities, and many cases are so complex and so hotly disputed that I have skirted the whole matter of subspecies or geographic
races, calling all willet willet, so to speak, despite the knowledge that the
western willet and eastern willet have long been treated as distinct, that
the average western bird is larger, and so forth. Until classification of
shorebirds is more advanced, almost anything one writes on their evolution and taxonomy may be out-of-date before it can be published; the
present chapter is not intended as an argument for any case but as an
evocation of exciting possibilities. (Parasitologists, for example, explain-
ing that birds acquired parasites before their evolution had gone very far,
and that these parasites evolved in company with their hosts, have suggested[90] that bird relationships may be clarified by close comparison of
feather lice or other creatures; parasites are so partial to their own hosts
that two whole genera of tapeworms are found in shorebirds only.)

Many shorebirds, to begin with, have no subspecies at all: such cos-
mopolitans as the sanderling and black-bellied plover, though scattered
across both hemispheres, have little or no morphological variation in
their populations. Ordinarily, this absence of subspecies would be considered sign of a static or senile form, lacking vitality, but shorebirds,
with their great powers of dispersal, are rarely exposed to the geographic
isolation necessary to the development of new races. The shorebirds have
little opportunity for adaptive radiation, a phenomenon in which a single species, arriving on a distant island, mountain top or other isolated
environment and finding there only a well-entrenched population of its
own ancestral stock with which it can neither compete nor interbreed,
radiates into markedly different forms to take advantage of new ecologies.

Historically, on the other hand, the shorebirds, like any other group,
might be called examples of adaptive radiation, since presumably all
shorebirds sprang from a single ancestor. One hypothesis[94] of shorebird

history runs approximately as follows: First, the ancestral species, evolving in the polar basin during an epoch of warm climate, flourished and became circumpolar. Then, an ice age drove this single species southward, and it fanned out into separate regions of the globe. These separate populations, cut off from one another down the centuries, were modified by differing ecologies and genetic divergence into geographic races or subspecies; eventually, as their differences increased, the races evolved into distinct species. A subsequent age of gentle climate encouraged some but not all of these new shorebirds to follow the retreating ice back toward the Arctic, where several species eventually became circumpolar; those which remained behind became the progenitors of the temperate and tropical forms such as the stilts and thick-knees. Again an ice age drove the northern species southward, and again the scattered populations were divided by isolation into new species. (One or more of the original species descended from the common ancestor may have already established its own genus, comprised of its descendant species.) A withdrawal of the glaciers at the end of the Pleistocene permitted some but not all of the modern shorebirds to return toward the Arctic, where a few, such as the northern phalarope and sanderling, again became circumpolar or nearly so. (Tropical and temperate families, as well as certain members of essentially northern families—cf. the Tahitian sandpiper—were once again left behind.) Theoretically, a new Ice Age would bring about a repetition of this process, and a further enlargement in the number of shorebird forms. All of this appears quite logical, but what did (and what might) actually happen remains wholly in the realm of speculation.

"Spatial isolation permits genetic divergence to continue until reproductive isolation is achieved."[109] For example, the minute morphological differences between races of the rock sandpiper, brought about by partial isolation, might eventually lead to major genetic divergence through mutations, followed by the emergence of a new species. At first it seems curious that the rock sandpiper, confined in breeding season to the region of the Bering Sea, has developed several races, while its sibling the purple sandpiper is uniform throughout a range which is nearly circum-

polar. But "in a large population subdivided into numerous partially isolated groups, both adaptive and non-adaptive differentiation is to be
expected: such conditions are most favorable for evolution."[13]

Like most geographic races, the races of the rock sandpiper are virtually indistinguishable in the field, and such distinctions as can be made
appear to most of us so trivial as to be unworthy of notice: The Russians,
indeed, dismiss the rock sandpiper itself as a race of the purple sandpiper. (One Russian authority[36] has declared that the Eskimo curlew is
only a race of the little curlew of Siberia: perhaps the former, as an
English writer suggested, has been saved from extinction by systematics.[31] In the hand, the Eskimo curlew can be identified by the hexagonal
reticulations on the back of the tarsi, but in the field the two are at least
as indistinguishable as the whimbrels of eastern Siberia and western
North America, which are considered races of a single species, and the
same Englishman, in a more recent publication,[81] seems to support the
Russian view that the Eskimo and little curlews are conspecific. The
question, like many questions of classification, is still open.)

Another dispute involves the long-billed dowitcher, *Limnodromus
scolopaceus,* and the short-billed dowitcher, *L. griseus scolopaceus,*
described in 1823 (from Long's expedition to the Rocky Mountains), is
generally agreed to be a larger, more richly colored bird, with a longer
bill, but these morphological differences are not usually sufficient to
qualify a form as a distinct species. Nevertheless, *scolopaceus* remained a
"good" species until 1931, despite the contempt in which it was held by
such naturalists as the sharp-tongued Dr. Coues, who declared that it
was "supposed to be rare or casual on the Atlantic Coast and declared to
be the only representative of the genus in the west—which would be
important if it were a fact."[22] Later authorities were also suspicious of
this bird, and in 1931 the American Ornithologists' Union demoted it
to subspecies, having been persuaded that a population of dowitchers
breeding in Alberta was intermediate between *griseus* and *scolopaceus,* and
that all three were therefore races of a single species.

But in 1957, the long-billed dowitcher was restored from *L. g.
scolopaceus* to plain *L. scolopaceus.* Researchers[83] have established to the

satisfaction of the AOU that the bill and legs of *scolopaceus* are longer than those of *griseus* owing to a habit of feeding in freshwater pools in preference to shallow tide flats; that *scolopaceus* is a tundra bird, breeding to the north and west of *griseus;* and that the separation of one species of dowitchers into two took place in the Pleistocene, when the population breeding in central and western Alaska and Siberia was cut off from the population to the south and east by southward-moving glaciers. And all this has taken place despite the fact that two centuries after the short-billed dowitcher was first reported, a nest of the "type" race of Labrador and Quebec has still to be described, although very young chicks have been located. (The first eggs of this nominate race may have been unofficially collected a half-century ago by Walter Raine, an oologist whose skilled egg-gathering for commercial gain had earned him the distrust of bird authorities. Perhaps to avoid the scholarly abuse that would have met an amateur's claim to the first eggs of *griseus,* he sold his two clutches quietly to a British collector. These Labrador clutches were subsequently compared with clutches from farther west: "the eggs were undoubtedly those of . . . *L. griseus.*"[7])

The Russians, in any case, remain unimpressed with the differences between the dowitchers, which they regard as geographic variations of a single species, *Macrorhamphus griseus.*

When geographic races of a species are linked by intergrading groups, the species is said to be continuous: even cosmopolitan and/or circumpolar species like the common snipe, the races of which extend around the world, may be continuous, or nearly so. (On the other hand, the races of the snowy plover, also cosmopolitan—this is disputed; some authorities give certain races full-species rank—are widely separated; in its strangely scattered populations, most of them nonmigratory, the snowy plover more closely resembles the glossy ibis than any other shorebird.) The semipalmated plover and the very similar ringed plover of Eurasia have complementary ranges which, taken together, encircle the globe, yet these siblings do not interbreed where the ranges overlap, in northeastern Baffin Island.

The whimbrel of North America presents a situation in which a single race, divided into eastern and western populations which remain separated all year-round, has nevertheless remained entirely uniform. The glacier theory (which may explain the evolution into separate species of the western and semipalmated sandpipers) is difficult to apply here, for the exact identity of the two whimbrel populations suggests that the separation is a recent one, far more recent than the Pleistocene. It has been supposed[100] that a Mississippi flyway whimbrel, linking the two populations, was exterminated during the commercial slaughters of 70 years ago which also destroyed the Eskimo curlew, and until a better is found, this seems a quite logical explanation, especially since, in the 19th century, the two species were often confounded, even by ornithologists. Or it may be that the whimbrel of the central continent had been displaced much earlier by the more numerous Eskimo curlew and is gradually reoccupying that territory now that the smaller bird has disappeared. In colonial times the rarest of our three curlews, the whimbrel, is now much the most common, and the reasons for this are fairly well established. Unlike *N. americanus,* it nests in the far north out of harm's way; unlike *N. borealis,* it has no dangerous overseas migration, nor did it ever travel in large flocks. And unlike both, it is wary. In recent years, at any rate, whimbrels have occurred regularly in the Mississippi Valley, and eventually all North American populations may be joined.

Eastern and western races of the dunlin, solitary sandpiper and long-billed curlew are linked by intermediate forms, but in all three, as in the willet and long-billed dowitcher, the western form is, on the average, larger. Why these western birds should average larger than the eastern is a question which naturalists have avoided, but the explanation, when it comes, may be as simple and indisputable as the glacier that split the dowitchers in two. (Alaskan mammals are almost invariably the largest individuals in their species, in apparent illustration of Bergmann's rule; perhaps the size of western shorebirds, which tend to nest somewhat farther north than do eastern forms of the same species, is another aspect of this phenomenon.)

The "red-backed sandpiper" of my childhood is now known by the

same common name as its Eurasian counterpart the dunlin; the change
represented no change in rank but simply a recent and laudable trend
among British and American naturalists to simplify bird nomenclature.
This is quite different from the talk of making all three oystercatchers of
the Northern Hemisphere—the black, American and Eurasian—a single
species; here the assumption is that the different degrees of white in their
plumages are racial rather than specific differences and that other distinctions are also quantitative rather than qualitative. The black oystercatcher shares the pink legs and the red-ringed yellow eyes of the American,
and these two, where their ranges overlap, have been known to interbreed. The Eurasian oystercatcher has red legs, while the legs of the New
World oystercatchers are pinkish white, but these different markings may
be relatively unimportant, since in color changes only a very few genes
are involved. "The resemblances between the Old- and New-World
white-breasted oyster-catchers become particularly significant when
plumage is considered in relation to age, for the American forms retain
as adults essentially the juvenal phase of the Old-World bird. . . . If we
place the richly marked Eurasian Oyster-catcher at the focus of a more or
less concentric series, and proceed eastward and southeastward through
and beyond the palearctic region, or southwestward across both continents of America, we find running through the successive races of oystercatchers a similar and progressive type of variation, which is correlated
with geographic distribution."[64] The black oystercatcher is less shy than
the American, and it has developed calks on its feet, an anatomical distinction which seems to have stemmed from an environmental one;
probably because of available foods on the Pacific coast, it prefers a rock
habitat to sand. Though "features directly selected by habitat are *not* of
generic value,"[28] the two oystercatchers of this continent will probably
be treated as distinct until more evidence to the contrary has been
brought forward.

Taxonomic disputes are not confined to subspecies and species; they
are, if anything, still more intense when it comes to the higher groupings. We have, for example, the checkered history of the sanderling,
which, on the basis of a shortish bill and the absence of hind toe, was

long classed among the plovers. The Chilean sandpiper—known in less hardheaded days as Mitchell's Slenderfoot—was also called a plover on the same grounds. Alexander Wilson, who perpetuated the sanderling convention, nonetheless spoke out against it:

> The present species, though possessing the build, general figure, manners, and voice of the sandpipers, feeding in the same way, and associating with these in particular, yet wanting the hind toe, has been classified with the Plovers, with whom, this single circumstance excepted, it has no one characteristic in common. Though we have not, in the present instance, presumed to alter this arrangement, yet it appears both reasonable and natural, that, where the specific characters of any birds seem to waver between two species, figure, voice and habits of the equivocal one should always be taken into consideration, and be allowed finally to determine the class to which it belongs. Had this rule been followed in the present instance, the bird we are now about to describe would undoubtedly have been classed with the Sandpipers.

Wilson's perception was precocious, for in the century after his death, the description of species remained a dry and arbitrary science, based on the real or imagined differences in the morphology and/or anatomy of museum specimens. Only recently has the study of comparative behavior brought systematics more nearly into balance: the surfbird, for example, looks like a sandpiper in every way, right down to the hind toe, and for many years was thought to be one. Yet both structure and behavior relate it more closely to the plovers, among which, for the nonce, it is usually placed.

"Classification into discrete groups is fairly easy at any one time, but it is not easy over long periods of time."[13] The evolutionary tree is more accurately conceived of as a bush—a dense bush, moreover, from which the whole base and the lower branches have been lost, leaving a mass of disconnected twigs and branches. *Presbyornis*, an Eocene form which vaguely links curlews and phalaropes, and *Rhegminornis*, a jaçana relative of Miocene Florida, are the only extinct shorebird families known:[43] Since the fossil record is so very fragmentary, a taxonomy which must be based in part on the pattern of extinct forms is dealing at best with probabilities. The surfbird, now the sole representative of its own genus, may be found to have been one of several species in a much larger genus, the other members of which are now extinct. Or a fossil plover may be discovered, with new findings, to have represented an entire genus, or even a family, in those early mornings of the world when the shorebird group was still confined to a few cranelike marsh birds.

Thus classification in terms of genus, family and order (and subgenus, superfamily, suborder—there are no limits to the zeal of the systematist when he is dealing with abstractions) is primarily a means of reducing to systematics the more than 8,000 bird species that fly the earth: the labels attached to every bird are mainly relative to other labels and are forever being changed by newer labelers. In the nineteenth century, the dowitchers were placed successively in *Limosa* (godwits), *Scolopax* (a former genus name for snipes) and *Ereunetes* (a genus of small sandpipers); in Russia today, the dowitcher is once again considered a kind of "snipelike godwit," a classification which certain parts of its anatomy support. But an anatomist's criteria for separate genus rank are not always the same as those of the morphologist or the behaviorist, and past criteria were in general so debatable that in the two decades preceding 1950 more than half of the bird genera of the world were eliminated. More have perished since: among the shorebirds, in recent years, *Erolia*, *Ereunetes* and *Crocethia* have all been incorporated in the genus *Calidris* and *Micropalama* (the stilt sandpiper may one day join them). The genus "is now defined not merely as a group of related species but as a group of species with similar ecology. When a species shifts into a major new ecological niche, the stage is set for the origin of a new genus."[60] Among behaviorists, this definition still leaves ample arena for dispute.

Even the family is no longer sacred. On the basis of comparative analysis of skull hinges, the family Phalaropodidae has been discarded by some 67 authorities who consider the phalaropes to be true sea sandpipers of the family Scolopacidae: One writer[91] suggests that they are "near allies" to the *Calidris*, differing mainly in such environmental characters as lobed feet and dense furry plumage, which may have little more generic value than the calks of the black oystercatcher. It appears, then, that only the species—the lowest rank in the taxonomic order of which all members are reproductively isolated from other living things—can be determined with much assurance. All groupings between the kingdom (we know the jaçana is an animal and not a plant) and the species (we know or think we know—the jaçana is so peculiar in every way that it is scarcely to be trusted—that the jaçana is a jaçana and does not interbreed with non-jaçanas)—are purely positional, the abstract inventions of man, and therefore open to revision. The groupings are based on the selection by a taxonomist of one or more characters allegedly shared by all members of that grouping, and they are valid only to the degree that other taxonomists choose to recognize them.

"I have long thought," said Charles Darwin in a letter, "that too much systematic work . . . somehow blunts the faculties."[24] It seems too bad, in any case, that so much energy is spent in taxonomic haggling, especially when more basic questions remain unanswered. And the taxonomist's job seems especially thankless when the factor of behavior is added to the rest. The black-bellied plover is often assigned to the genus *Pluvialis* of the goldens, despite marked morphological discrepancies, including the presence in the black-belly of a rudimentary hind toe. But that hind toe is considered a superficial character, and the contrast in ecology and behavior is probably more significant. The black-belly is wary, an indifferent formation flyer, with a liking for loose flocks, longshore habitats, late coastal migration and the company of knots; the tendencies of the golden, which are just the reverse, include field habitats and a marked avoidance of knot company. Furthermore, young blackbellies, like most bird young, are relatively tame, while old-time accounts of shorebird gunning all attest that young goldens were wary and difficult to shoot, far more so than their parents, in direct contravention of our cherished notions in regard to the wisdom of our elders. (One wonders if the adult birds, with their habit of Eskimo curlew company, were not led to their doom by that still-more innocent and ill-fated crea-ture which was said to have been the leader of their common flocks.).

DUNLIN

RUFF AND REEVE

7

Perhaps no one dreamed of Snipe an hour ago, the air seemed empty of such as they; but as soon as the dusk begins, so that a bird's flight is concealed, you hear this peculiar spirit-suggesting sound, now heard through and above the evening din of the village.

—*Thoreau*, Walden

THE VOICE OF the dunlin, drifted down the tundras of the northern world from Greenland west to Somerset Island, and from Ireland eastward to Alaska, has been likened to the tinkling of ice in water. The barrens have been wakened from the silences of winter by an amorous outcry carried far and wide on the arctic wind, and even the rock and least sandpipers, which share parts of the dunlin's range, have spring voices more melodious than the gritty sounds that these birds make in the remainder of the year.

The dunlin, one of the first wind birds in the Arctic, is often seen picking around bleak tundra ponds that are still locked in ice. A set of dunlin eggs recorded in Alaska late in May is an early one indeed, for the last ice and raw weather will often inhibit courtship or postpone it; if the weather is bad enough, bird migrants may reflock again, even after courtship has begun, and fly southward for a few hours or even a few days, in a setback known as reverse migration. (Reverse migration does not seem to account for a well-documented[113] sighting of flocks of small peep sandpipers, fifty to several hundred per flock, observed 600 miles east of New York, flying strongly, and making no attempt to alight on shipboard; though the month was May, they were not headed north toward their breeding grounds, but southeast by east, toward Africa.)

The first migrants—usually lone males—drop down each day and night from the southern stars. Ruddy turnstones, which may complete an annual migration north but fail to breed, sometimes arrive in separate flocks of cocks and hens, whereas the Baird's sandpiper and the golden plover (and perhaps others—little is known of this stage of the mating cycle) may have paired before arrival. The birds recover quickly from the rigors of their flight, and within a few hours or a few days, depending on conditions, are fat and rich-feathered again, swollen with life and song.

The courtship of the shorebird is an extravagant expression of the intensity of its existence. For the brief period of reproduction, an enormous amount of energy has been accumulated which must be spent in a short time, and usually is—a Eurasian woodcock has been known[109] to sacrifice one seventh of its total weight before its abandon ran its course. But often the female birds are tardy, or an excess of other males of its own species must be dealt with, and in this frustrating period its excess energies are usually spent in song, mock fighting and territorial display.

The defense of territory is ordinarily the foundation for all activities within the breeding cycle.

> The theory of territory in bird life is briefly this: that pairs are spaced through the pugnacity of males towards others of their own species and sex; that song and display of plumage and other signals are a warning to other males and an invitation to a female; that males fight primarily for territory and not over mates; that the owner of the territory is nearly invincible in his territory; and finally, that birds which fail to obtain terri-

tory form a reserve supply from which replacements come in case of death to owners of territory.[67]

That certain sandpipers exhibit little territoriality, and that the red and northern phalaropes will often fight *outside* the territory[102] suggests that the role of territory can be overemphasized; still, it is of great importance. Territorial sequestration is chiefly a defense against other breeding pairs of the same species: Where energies are limited and time is short, it insures against the endless disorder of confrontations and chronic fighting, as well as overcrowding and the contagion of disease; it also promotes stability and knowledge of one's own ground and natural resources in time of stress, a crucial advantage in foul weather.

Since territories are contested before they are established, they forward natural selection, the "survival of the fittest"; in forcing fringe birds into new habitats at the outer limits of the range, they encourage geographic expansion, adaptability and even the evolution of new species.

The most easily defended territory would be circular in shape, with the nest site somewhere near the center; where circumstances permit, variations on this arrangement are the rule. In crowded habitats, territories become increasingly irregular, being squashed against, between, and around one another like parts of a jigsaw puzzle. Sometimes an irregular shape is caused by the use of a natural boundary like a ridge or pond, and sometimes by the loss of a piece of territory to a stronger neighbor: with the arrival of new birds and population pressures, a given territory may shrink from a bold domain to a bent corner. The size of the territory may also depend on its owner's habits and pugnacity, and on the use to which the territory will be put: it may vary from the few square feet of a colonial nester like the avocet—which, being colonial, fights customarily in defense of its female, rather than in defense of territory, and obtains both food and nesting materials elsewhere—to the several acres ordinarily established by the whimbrel.

Territories are defended with a vigor which varies markedly from species to species. Killdeer are so zealous in territorial defense that even a sparrow, venturing too near, may expose itself to bodily attack, whereas willets, though vociferous, tend to be rather slipshod about boundaries and rarely enter into actual combat. The willet serves notice on all interlopers by circling high into the air, wings flickering, shrieking, *"Pill-will-willet!"*; on the ground, it may bristle fearsomely, to increase its size.[107] Because of the overwhelming psychological advantage possessed by the home bird, loud vocal threat is usually an adequate defense against an invading male of the same species, unless that male is pursuing a strayed hen; territorial borders may be intricate, and the hens sometimes take a while to get them straight. (Among Eurasian oystercatchers, should a courting male be bothered by a rival cock, he begins "a kind of mimicry of the interloper, and apparently this works as well as fighting, the transgressor usually being forced to leave."[35])

The habitats chosen by spring shorebirds are extremely various. Grassland or prairie is favored by some, shores and marshes attract others. The surfbird, wandering tattler and bristle-thighed curlew like high alpine situations. Deciduous woods are the haunt of the woodcock, coniferous forest (and particularly spruce muskeg) the haven of such sandpipers as the Hudsonian godwit and the whimbrel. But more than half of all North American shorebird species return yearly to the northern tundra.

The tundra is a vast, rank pasture of mosses, lichens, sedge grass, sphagnum, dwarf willow and bright flowers, girdling the northern world between boreal forest and perpetual snow. Its frozen subsoil, preventing seepage of the melted frosts, insures the formation every spring of myriad ponds and pools. These wetlands swarm with crane flies and caddis flies, beetles, mosquitoes, aquatic midges, spiders and other small invertebrates, and the water birds which time their migrations to take advantage of the insect cycles are the dominant wildlife. There are few native predators—the nesting birds have more to fear from the jaegers that flew north with them than from the snowy owls and bears and Arctic foxes. In the endless light and provender of the midnight sun, reproduction is markedly accelerated, and the young are so quickly self-sufficient that many of the parent birds are headed south once more by early summer. Thus the most vulnerable period of the young is limited to a few weeks.

A characteristic of the tundra is an almost total lack of elevated perches: this is the barren ground, and except for thin lines of dwarf willow and alder in the river bottoms and depressions, it is treeless. Few songbirds nest upon the tundra, and those that do, like the longspurs and snow buntings, sing most commonly while on the wing; the shorebirds do the same.

In the thousands of miles of the flight north, the communal voice of the speeding birds has called the strays back from the void and held the flocks together; at the stopping points and on the tundras, that voice has warned of gyrfalcons and jaegers. But the role of the voice in reproduction is the foremost of its functions: the phenomenon of voice, in frogs and men as well as birds, originated as an enticement to copulation. In proclaiming the species of the singer, it helps insure against weak hybrid forms; at the same time, it serves warning on competitors of the same species to stay clear. In attracting a listener of the other sex, in conveying the urgency that stimulates ovulation and other appropriate reaction and as call and recognition notes within its family, the voice advances the regeneration of the species.

The wind birds are not credited with the ability to sing, a disgrace that they share with all nonmembers of the Passeriformes, or perching birds—the so-called songbirds. Yet the calls of shorebirds are often more melodious than the songs of songbirds. Since songbirds and non-songbirds use their voices for the same purposes, and since birdsong is a functional activity, seldom if ever performed for pleasure, the term "songbird" becomes even more unreliable than the term "shorebird." Any man who, hearing the spring fluting of the upland sandpiper as it drifts down through the morning over a sunny meadow, finds this beautiful sound less songlike than that of the song sparrow on the fence below, is making a mysterious distinction. "First a few notes, like water gurgling from a large bottle, then comes the loud *whip-whel-ee-you,* long drawn out and weirdly thrilling."[8] (In the days when the upland sandpiper was a common bird on the Long Island moors, Mackay shot seven near Sagaponack, but by 1916 the species was already scarce: "The merest remnant of Bartramian sandpipers yet keeps a foothold at the extreme eastern end

of the island."[69] One morning in the mists of May I heard it passing overhead, but I have never seen it on Long Island. I first watched and listened
to the upland sandpiper in the old Common Pasture at Newburyport,
and the memory of it makes my temples tingle to this day.)

Bird voices are crucial to the survival of the species, though the bird
does not use its voice toward some foreseen end; rather, it cries out in instinctive response to certain stimuli. The vitalists would dispute such
views, which have been chosen, not to dismiss all nonfunctional bird behavior, but because, in the absence of good evidence, the mechanistic attitude seems more responsible. Yet one may suppose, for want of a functional explanation, that the yellowlegs soars high in the blue skies of
summer because it enjoys doing so, and that the air tag witnessed[4] in the
black-necked stilt, in which, when the bird pursued is overtaken by its
companions, another becomes "it," is largely if not entirely play. (A kind
of catch-as-catch-can has also been observed in the southern lapwing of
the Argentine: "I was one day watching a flock of plovers, quietly feeding on the ground, when, in a moment, all the birds were seized by a
joyous madness, and each one, after making a vigorous peck at his nearest neighbor, began wildly running about, each trying in passing to peck
other birds, while seeking by means of quick doublings to escape being
pecked in turn."[45])

Whatever the purpose, shorebirds and others depend for their vocal
effects on the avian apparatus called the syrinx. The syrinx corresponds
to the larynx in mammals, but it is located at the *lower* end of the tra-
chea, which serves it as a sort of resonating tube; its versatility largely depends on the number of contracting muscles and vocal membranes,
though some species in which these parts are well represented possess
voices of singular dullness.

At least one authority[8] maintains that shorebird voices can be related
to habitat: thus, the snipe's low guttural *scaip* well suits the sequestered
bogs which it prefers, where voices of frog and heron resound continu-
ally. Except in breeding season, the woodcock of the alder swamp
confines itself to a low *peent,* as if it were trying to clear its bill of mud,
and the pectoral sandpiper was known locally on Long Island as the

"krieker," after the low reedy sounds that it emits in the dank salt meadows of its preference. These voices contrast strangely with the shrill cries and clear whistles heard on the flats and shore, and so does the "loud scream"[32] of the long-billed curlew, which is entirely out of harmony with any habitat that one can think of.

The link between voice and habitat seems as natural as the link between habitat and coloring, but with shorebirds there are always exceptions. The knot, a bird addicted to the open coasts, has a voice as boggish as that of the woodcock, while most peep are restricted to small sounds which have been likened, accurately, to the noise of pebbles being rubbed together. Away from home, the Hudsonian godwit rarely makes a sound of any kind. Yet all of these birds, in breeding season, do much better. The *poor-me* of the knot, ringing over the snow fields of the tundra, is one of the loveliest of wind-bird songs, and the cry of the Hudsonian godwit one of the loudest.

In the great majority of shorebirds, the sexes are scarcely distinguishable in the field, even among those species in which the spring plumage differs markedly from winter dress. In the Hudsonian godwit, however, the seasonal red-browns of the male and female plumages are distinguishable, and the spring male has more white in his back feathers. The phalaropes, too, are sexually dimorphic, though the differences between male and female are not at all what one would expect; the male phalarope is not larger and more gaudy than his mate, as in most birds, but exactly the reverse, a chagrin he shares with the male jaçana.

Because the sexes are similar in most species, the voice is more important than spring plumage as a secondary sex character (the unique primary character, and quite rightly, is the gonad), since it reveals not only individual but sexual identity. In many shorebirds, cock and hen may both add voices to the din—not surprisingly, since the shorebirds are notoriously inconsistent in regard to the roles of the sexes, not only in courtship but in nesting.

Certain species, although anxious for a hearing, do not use the syrinx to achieve their finest sound effects. The lapwing, an occasional visitor from Europe, uses its wing quills to produce an unmusical "chattering" effect much to the liking of its females, to judge from the abundance of this bird throughout its range. (But William Blake was so concerned about the lapwing that he wrote a poem beginning, "O lapwing, thou fliest round the heath, Nor seest the net that is spread beneath. . . .") The woodcock, with the three stiff narrow feathers of its outer primaries, and the snipe, with the lateral feathers of its short tail, produce analogous but dissimilar sounds best known as "feather music," and the black turnstone is comparably gifted, filling the air over its breeding grounds on the Alaskan coast with a mighty *zum-zum-zum*.

As the male woodcock, like a love-struck leaf, flutters earthward for the benefit of its intended, the air forced past its quills produces an eerie quavering; the aerial evolutions of the snipe are accompanied by fantastic loud, wild whifflings. In its passion, the snipe may fly short distances upside down, but its most stirring effects are not attained until its high-altitude maneuvers are completed; it now hurtles earthward as if bent on the total destruction of all beneath, traveling with such speed and force that its passage creates an awesome *zoom* or *boom*. In this sport, the snipe is tireless: one rainy June in the Northwest Territories, in the high moose-and-caribou country north of Ross River, I watched snipe careen through the huge gray skies for long days at a time, waking the heavens with the sound that has caused this shy creature to be known in Europe as the "thunderbird."

Unlike those species which declare themselves on high, the Baird's sandpiper conducts itself discreetly, executing its "butterfly" flight at a low altitude over the female's head. Variations on this slow flitting or shivering flight are practiced by most courting shorebirds (though for the Wilson's plover and the buff-breasted sandpiper, no courting flight of any kind has been reported); so is wild zigzag pursuit of one sex by the other. In several species, both sexes participate in an aerial courtship flight, which, among killdeer at least, may last for an hour or more. There is also a kind of frantic hovering, pronounced in the Wilson's phalarope and the upland and stilt sandpipers, the last of which, in these exalted moments, permits itself a "donkey-like hee-haw";[40] the white-rumped sandpiper may hover at 100 feet for as long as 20 minutes.[99]

Males of the great snipe of Eurasia (*Capella media*) display together in a line, bills chattering and feathers snapping, and may spar a bit in a ritualized sort of way.[114] The willet, once its passions are engaged, displays a fine high-stepping strut, and it also lifts its brilliant wing in amorous display, a habit shared, in spite of less flashy equipment, by the purple, the Baird's and the buff-breasted sandpiper. The willet's wing has an auxiliary use as a flocking or flight signal,[107] and the purple sandpiper, it appears, may raise its wing in simple greeting, but the wing display serves ordinarily as a deterrent to other males and as an attraction to the females. That its role as deterrent is the more important of the two is suggested by the behavior of the buff-breast. Like the rest, the buff-breast lifts a single wing, or sometimes two, at which point it runs about as if giddy with pride in its silver wing lining. Yet sometimes it displays in perfect solitude, in silence, as if practicing for some dread fray which awaits it in the future, and often it performs for the edification of other males, and even other species, rather than for its females, which customarily pay no attention to it whatsoever. As if downcast by such indifference, the buff-breast may perform its courtship while standing half-hidden in a hole.[79] Similarly, in the avocet, the idle males "stand in little groups and all talk at once. . . . A great deal of bowing and posing and running around each other takes place, and a variety of beautiful attitudes are assumed."[105]

Paired short-billed dowitchers sing sweetly and bill tenderly like pigeons, the cock of the long-billed curlew strokes the hen with his magnificent proboscis, and even the ruddy turnstone, which largely dispenses with display, may "comb" his partner's head feathers with his bill.[74] The sanderling, on the other hand, has no finesse at all. In this species, tender behavior and an attractive voice are replaced by haste and a coarse kind of "frog song"; its brusque attitude is impartially extended to mate and enemy alike.

> The male which had been standing close by ran and thrust his bill
> down beside her. . . . Then he stood on her back, stepped off and deliber-
> ately eased her out of the scrape with his bill and forehead thrust beneath

her belly. Both then ran off side by side with bodies pressed together and rubbing vigorously. Having run some 10 feet, the male lowered his head and pressed his bill forcibly against the breast of the female, immediately stopping her. She stood still and copulation followed.[75]

The pectoral sandpiper, over its long evolutionary course, has developed a throat of flaccid, vascularized tissue that transforms an otherwise indifferent voice into an awesome reverberation. On the ground, it huffs like a tiny turkey, and once aloft, sets sail across the tundra with head thrown back and tail straight down, uttering "queer groaning and hooting noises"[99] as it goes, and descending once more before its hen like a visitation.

The male white-rumped sandpiper develops an enlarged throat in breeding season, and it, too, has a weak pair-bond, paying close attention to passing females of its own and other species and little, if any, to the domestic activities of its mate; whether this is a sign of close phylogenetic relationship to the pectoral rather than parallel evolution is not yet known.[77] But the buff-breasted sandpiper, closely related to neither, has a vascularized throat as well as a tendency to polygamy, and like the cock white-rump, ignores the pair-bond once the egg-laying is over.[98]

As noted above, the hen buff-breast pays little attention to her cock, and similarly, the hen pectoral is so little attached to her errant mate that she scarcely glances at his puffs and hootings (inflated male pectorals, as if chagrined, can snap shut in seconds), often abandoning the vicinity of their alliance to make her nest. The still-more spectacular displays and posturing of the ruff, sometimes culminating in actual battle, may advance its chances not at all in the eyes of the female ruff, known as the reeve.

Though it has never been known to nest in North America, the ruff has turned up so regularly on the Atlantic Coast and in Alaska that a first nesting record is a distinct possibility: there were 30 North American records of the ruff in 1963 alone. This peculiar bird is on its best behavior here: it "seems to be silent . . . as a rule, walks quite erect, rather deliberately, and probes in the mud for its food. . . ."[32] The ruff is still more specialized than the pectoral sandpiper. Because neither confines it-self to a single mate during the course of a given breeding season, and because the cock pectoral and ruff are unusual among shorebirds in be-ing much larger than their hens', it has been suggested[84] that the pec-toral's curious behavior may be a sign of an evolutionary progress toward the male dancing ground, or lek, system of the ruff.

The ruff is rare among shorebirds in being varicolored, or polymor-phic; in nuptial feathering, the cock displays a nice range of hues, both on its "cape" and in the odd ruff about its neck, which may come in al-most any color from white to red to brown or black. (Though "stable polymorphism" of this kind—seen also in periwinkles and certain fish and insects—is not well understood, it may be a sign that the genes in-volved are still in the process of selection.[13]) To these adornments, the ruff in breeding season goes about with a bare face, which is decorated during this period with bright red tubercles, or "warts." He repairs to the same dancing ground, year after year, and there struts, twirls and pos-tures on his mound or stamping area and fights with others of his gor-geous sex by leaping high into the air or seizing another's ruff in antic jealousy; if no reeve is in the offing, he may make a fine display to a clod of turf. Ruff behavior has so impressed the Chukchi Indians of Siberia that they have celebrated it in an imitative dance, like the prairie-chicken dances of our Plains tribes.

Ruffs and reeves travel in bachelor flocks all year, but the sexes draw near in breeding season and one or more reeves may turn up at the danc-ing ground and loiter in the nearby grass, looking restless. At the conclu-sion of a fight, while the ruffs run wildly to and fro, the reeve steps into view, whereupon the obsequious ruffs crouch low in supplication, wings partially spread, heads bowed, to await her choice. Flashy appearance, to the reeve, counts for far more than fighting heart, and she is as like as not to nibble at the rumpled neck display, not of the victor, but of the loser, in sign of sexual acquiescence, a perversity which one is tempted to hold responsible for the large incidence of homosexuality found in this species. In fact, homosexuality and promiscuity are the vices of both sexes, a circumstance further exemplified in the reeve's habit of bestowing her favors in quick succession not only upon the ruff of her choice but on the next ruff (or reeve) in line, as well as in the unmasculine attitudes of the rejected ruffs, which, unlike cock birds that lack dancing grounds, stand by resignedly during mating instead of rushing forth to interfere. The only time that a rival is interrupted is when a loose male, flapping skittishly about, collides by accident with the partners. This chaotic state of affairs is hardly improved by the indiscriminate nature of ruff passions, which have caused it to mount tufts of grass with every sign of ardor, not to speak of consenting males and even stuffed specimens of its own kind placed nearby for purpose of experiment. In truth, the firm silence it maintains on almost all occasions is the one thing that can be shown in praise of the dignity of *Philomachus pugnax.*

To do it justice, the ruff is not alone in its weakness for copulation with stuffed specimens: the tendency has been noted[71] in wrens and other birds in which—unlike the ruff—the sexes appear identical. Unless given those clues of voice and behavior which stuffed specimens are unable to provide, many birds have difficulty in distinguishing cock from hen, and must proceed on a trial-and-error basis, taking the risk that their finest displays and posturing may well be met with indifference, or even a rude assault. The stuffed specimen, which displays a pleasing submissiveness by neither attacking nor moving off, is no doubt gratifying to the reeling cock, half-blind and stupid with emotion, and may be reduced to a feathered shambles before any decline occurs in the enthusiasm of its admirer.

Many shorebird species, while not fighters of the caliber of *P. pugnax,* will assuage their passions in a kind of mock combat should their vocal and display warnings go unheeded. The avocet, aroused, may throw straws and shells all over the place, and an oystercatcher has been seen to attack a bush. The black-necked stilt can become so overwrought that it will lay its head among its back feathers, as if asleep, for want of a better way to vent its feelings. (This phenomenon, in which an entirely inappropriate course of action gives sign of repressed emotion, is called "displacement activity," and is dealt with later in more detail.) The embattled avocet, on the other hand, may decide all of a sudden to lie down.

Whether it is anxious to make peace or is overcome by some sort of infe-
riorism is not known, but either way it spares itself a thrashing.

Since the ruff does not appear to defend territories (unless its small
space in the lek is considered territory), it is an exception to the theory
that spring display is chiefly a means of territorial defense: that is, the
showy willet wing, the puffed-out collar of the Wilson's plover are
thought to warn as well as win, whereas the ruff concerns itself exclusively with winning.

Until the first ruff struts its mound in North America, the New
World will have no shorebird so abandoned in its breeding habits. Plain
promiscuity, however, has been laid at the door of the woodcock, which
depends on roadways or other bare ground to show off its portly and
short-legged little body. Here, as an enticement to idle hens, it parades
like a tiny peacock, bowing and puffing and raising its bill toward the
heavens as it forces its head back, the better to display its chest; whereupon, rendered blind by its own pomp, it may stumble ignominiously,
or trip on sticks.

Promiscuity and the absence of true pair formation are thought to
encourage hybridization, to which there are other barriers to hybridization besides mutual infertility—differing breeding periods and ecologies,
mechanical obstacles and so forth. Among these, behavioral differences
are by no means the least important. While for the reeve the extravagan-
zas of the ruff are probably necessary to set her own reproductive se-
quence into motion, females of a more conservative species, far from being compromised by his exotic courtship, might feel impelled to flee.
With the possible exception of the mysterious Cooper's sandpiper (perhaps an aberrant pectoral, or knot; the unique specimen was taken on
Long Island in May 1833), no hybrid shorebird has ever been recorded
in North America, although in Europe an interspecific pairing of the
Eurasian curlew and the whimbrel has been reported.[72]

The mating that brings all this courtship to an end can incite the
other pairs in the vicinity to like behavior: multiple copulations, which

reach spectacular proportions among such colonial shorebirds as the avocet, are a survival adaptation in that they synchronize the breeding cycle
of the population and thereby reduce to the minimum the period of its
nesting vulnerability.

In the ensuing love feast, all but a few of the birds which have partic-
ipated in the courtships are involved. The ruddy turnstone may be star-
tled into copulation by a passing boat or airplane, or even by a hail-
storm,[3] but usually the sex act needs no goads. The Eurasian curlew, in
fact, has been seen to attempt aerial coition.[114] The willet, should his
mate tilt forward in response to all his wing-waving, mounts and copu-
lates without further ado, emitting a kind of jaunty clicking, as if snapping unseen fingers; the female, in these moments, has been heard to
give small grunted exclamations.[107] However, she tires of their intimacy
before he does. Sometimes she brings matters to a sudden end by throw-
ing her partner forward over her shoulder, upon which, agitated, he may
engage her in a kind of roughhouse. In the Wilson's plover, "when ready
for copulation, the female postures before the male, often moving ahead
of him if he turns away. She crouches and spreads her wings slightly. The
male walks up behind her, and for a little time, perhaps a minute or so,
marks time with a sort of 'goose step,' lifting each foot alternately back
and forth in the same place. . . ."[104]

Mating may take place several times a day for several days and may
continue intermittently, among killdeers, at least, even after incubation
has begun.

The long-billed dowitcher, unlike man, behaves in a joyful manner
after mating. "Hovering upon quivering wings, the bird pours forth a
lisping but energetic and frequently musical song, which can be very im-
perfectly expressed by the syllables *peet-peet; pee-ter wee-too; wee-too; pee-
ter-wee-too; pee-ter-wee-too; wee-too; wee-too.*"[8] In the black oystercatcher,
on the other hand, there appears to be little animation, either before or
after: The cock has been observed to "fly onto the hen's back from a distance. . . . The hen turned her head to look at the cock on her back. . . ."
Afterward, "both began preening as if nothing had occurred."[108] And the
hen of the northern phalarope, in the manner of certain spiders, may ac-

tually *attack* her mate after he mounts her, as if to remind him of his place.[101]

The weak and immature are turned away, as in mankind, and so are the crippled birds, and the abnormal. Individuals whose plumage has been altered by mutation or accident fare very poorly, as do albino deer and other aberrant creatures. But conformism is more healthy in birds than it is in man: birds not of a feather are out of harmony with their surroundings, and hence conspicuous, and hence a danger to their circle of acquaintance. Also, the regeneration of physically defective individuals could lead to degeneration of the species, as *H. sapiens* is learning to his cost with every advance of medical science. Even a bird that suffers injury after the pair-bond has been formed may find itself speedily rejected: In experiments with the *Halsbandregenpfeifer*, as the ringed plover is known in Germany, it was observed[50] that a bird which accidentally lost its foot was summarily abandoned by its mate. Nothing daunted, it located another one-footed individual and raised a brood of two-footed *Halsbandregenpfeifer.*

Besides the woodcock, with its loose ways, several other shorebirds have singular, or rather plural, family arrangements. Oystercatchers, though thought to pair for life, are often promiscuous within the pair-bond and may establish a *ménage à trois,* in which the third bird, usually a cock, assists his colleague by helping to serenade the hen in a three-way "piping ceremony," and perhaps in more intimate ways as well; he remains one of the family throughout the incubation. (But two of the pipers may suddenly rush about shoulder to shoulder, crowding their erstwhile comrade with such an excess of piping and commotion that, made to feel nervous and superfluous, he goes away.) Among black oystercatchers, intruders of the same species are not always assaulted, but may be "bowed off" ceremoniously with piping. They also engage in "flight piping," or *Flugbalz.*[108]

Similarly, in the southern lapwing of Patagonia, "one . . . will leave its mate and visit another pair in their territory and lead them in a ceremonial musical march; then return to its own holding to receive a visitor later on."[3]

The accommodations of the oystercatcher fall short of those attributed to phalaropes, in which one female may be attended by several
males, or vice versa. In the phalaropes—and the jaçanas, and the painted
snipes of the Southern Hemisphere—is found an ultimate expression of
the reversal of the sex roles: the hens are not only larger and more
brightly plumaged, but they conduct the entire courtship cycle from
start to finish, pausing only to lay the eggs. (The hen of the Old World
painted snipe, *R. benghalensis,* has a "deep and resonant" voice, whereas
the voice of her mate has been described as a "mere chirp."[35]) It is the
hen phalarope that displays and defends the territory, and courts, harries
and pursues the shrinking cock, which often flees the thumps and
nudges of its gaudy mate. "Twice I observed, how the male hid himself
between the tufts of vegetation, lying motionless with his head in a little
hole, the females walking nervously with outstretched neck in his neigh-
borhood, apparently searching for him."[101]

The mating of the northern phalarope ordinarily takes place on the
surface of the water. The hen of this species—which in her need has
been seen to display to a lapland longspur—will sometimes prostrate
herself before the male, so anxious is she for his service, the male is at
first rather timid and reluctant, but soon gets the hang of the thing and
may then become promiscuous. In both the Wilson's and the northern
phalarope, the males tend the nest and rear the young without assistance
from the mother; both are dowdy in appearance, to escape detection as
they go about their domestic duties. Idle hens of the Wilson's phalarope,
gallivanting in flocks, have been seen[74] to consort with handsome drakes
while their drab cocks and ducks minded the nests.

The phalaropes have carried their exchange of roles as far as their
anatomy will permit, and other shorebirds share their tendencies to a degree. In a number of sandpipers, the females are larger than the males
(though not more brightly plumaged: it is mainly in birds that mate and
part, such as the ruff and the pectoral sandpiper, that one finds not only
bold ornaments and colors, but striking somatic differences between the
sexes[4]), and in others, the bills of the females are longer. Female
courtship is practiced by the spotted sandpiper, and male incubation of

the eggs by numerous species which are otherwise traditionally oriented: the males of several sandpiper species are more attentive than their females to the young.

The plovers as a family are more staid in their deportment. In most plovers—the dotterel, a Eurasian species nesting uncommonly in Alaska, is an exception—and in certain sandpipers, the male and female share the incubation and the care of the young: among golden plovers, the male is thought to set by day, the hen at night.[101] In the long-billed dowitcher, the hen at first helps with the incubation but later tires of it and goes away, and in other species, too, one mate or the other does most of the incubation, a precaution taken by many ground-nesting birds against undue activity in the vicinity of the nest.

Oblivious of all this sexual equivocation is the brisk, no-nonsense ruddy turnstone, the male of which, as one might expect, is the more boldly colored, and his voice the louder; the black turnstone of the Pacific Coast is cast in the same mold. The ruddy turnstone has traveled far into the north, and wastes little time on dalliance; it dispenses with song flight entirely.[91] Under luminous skies of the aurora borealis, this squat and hardy bird gets on about the work of love in a silent, implacable manner, looking neither to the left nor the right.

PURPLE SANDPIPER

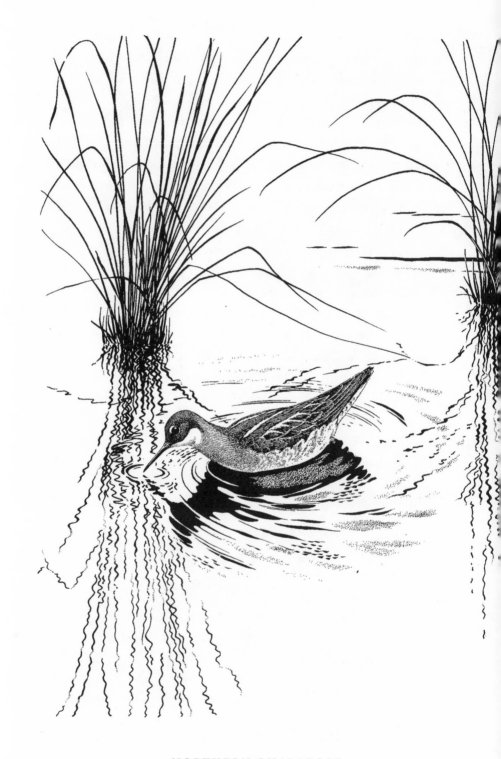

NORTHERN PHALAROPE

8

The ecstatic upland plover, hovering overhead, poured praises on something perfect: perhaps the eggs, perhaps the shadows, or perhaps the haze of pink phlox that lay on the prairie.

—*Aldo Leopold*, A Sand County Almanac

I N 1909, Admiral Peary, journeying homeward from his discovery of the North Pole, found in Grinnell Land, in north Ellesmere Island, the first knot nests ever seen by man. In ornithological circles this discovery was scarcely less momentous than the one he had made en route, for the nest of the knot had been hunted assiduously for half a century. (Arctic explorers, observing knots feeding near tundra pools, had mistakenly assumed that the nests must lie in the nearby grass; as it turned out, knots usually nest on high rock shale far from the water, a ground which affords them perfect camouflage.)

Nests of the wandering tattler and surfbird, in the mountains of Alaska, remained unknown until 1912 and 1926, and that of the bristle-thighed curlew, on upland tundra inland from the mouth of the Yukon, was located finally in 1948, nearly two centuries after the species was made known to science by Captain Cook. (The marbled murrelet, a Charadriiform of the auk family and a relatively common bird of the Pacific coast, makes the last nest still undiscovered in North America. Ordinarily, the auks are ground-nesters, but a marbled murrelet of eastern Siberia has recently been apprehended on a clump of lichen in a larch tree as it was settling on its own egg; presumably it indulges the same habit in British Columbia and/or southern Alaska.)

The solitary sandpiper confounded seekers of its nest for nearly a century. On June 16, 1903, a settler in what is now Alberta saw a strange bird fly to a robin's nest, 15 feet up in a tamarack, where he discovered the first eggs of the solitary sandpiper ever recorded. The find was surprising, yet it seems curious that ornithologists of the period were so taken aback, since the green sandpiper of Europe, already recognized as a close relative of *Tringa solitaria*, was celebrated as a tree-nester, and so was the European wood sandpiper. (In this last species, the habit is the more remarkable because so singular and at the same time not invariable—as if ovenbirds sometimes but not always constructed ovens.) Since 1903, many clutches have been found, most often in deserted nests of the rusty blackbird, cedar waxwing and gray jay; sometimes these nests are 40 feet above the ground.

Shorebirds exhibit a wide range of tastes in nest sites, even within the limited choice of habitats of the far north. A number like wet marshy ground, while others seek dry upland—bare, stony or heath and rocks, depending on the species. The surfbird inhabits rock slides, the black-bellied and golden plovers like lichen- or moss-covered tundra and the wandering tattler likes gravel bars in mountain river beds above tree line. There is scarcely a species, in fact, in which a unique preference in nesting habitat is not discernible: even the spotted sandpiper, for all its versatility, usually nests in the vicinity of fresh water.

Certain associations have been noted among shorebirds. Where their ranges overlap, the piping plover often nests in the company of least terns; this is as true on inland waters of the western states as it is on the open dunes at Sagaponack. Whether plover and tern like identical habitats, or whether some interdependence has been formed is still not known. The black oystercatcher (*H. ater*) of Patagonia will nest side-by-side with the black-backed gull; despite the bad reputation of that species: In this way, the oystercatchers obtain commensal protection from the gulls, which refrain from piracy within the boundaries of their own colony.[19] For the same reason, the ruddy turnstones of Sweden and Finland nest almost exclusively in the colonies of gulls and terns. The northern phalaropes of Iceland often nest right next to ptarmigan, which defend the homes of their small associates in the course of defending their own.[93]

In Iceland, too, the breeding dunlin associates so closely with the golden plover (this "greater or Eurasian" golden plover is sometimes classified as a distinct species, *P. apricaria*) that the dunlin is known there as the "plover's slave." Both species have black bellies in breeding season, but as the dunlin also seeks out purple sandpipers, and in one instance[93] became strongly attached to an Arctic tern, some other reason for its sociability must be sought.

Avocets will often nest in large polyglot colonies of ducks and gulls and terns; long-billed curlews are sometimes found in mixed colonies with marbled godwits. These curlews have been known to share not only territory but the nest itself with another pair of their own species, all four parents tending the eggs and young, and at least one pair has shared its nest successfully with willets. The bar-tailed godwit of Eurasia and Alaska may also be of sociable disposition, since a case is known of four godwit eggs laid directly on top of five eggs of the willow ptarmigan. The ptarmigan had no patience with this arrangement and departed, and the godwit apparently lost faith in it as well, for the nest was abandoned soon thereafter.

The jaçana is unique among North American shorebirds in its habitual construction of a true nest—a nest, moreover, which is designed to float. Most shorebird nests are nothing else than a vague depression or scrape on the open ground, barely deep enough to hold the eggs in a tight cluster. Yet this primitivism abets the survival of both eggs and young. First of all, in the short summer of the Arctic, precious days would be lost in nest construction. Also, on the open ground, when the eggs are well camouflaged, the barest of nests is the most obscure; an elaborate nest would not only be noticeable during incubation, but it would draw the attention of predators to young in the near vicinity. Even the woodcock, with a wealth of nesting materials at its disposal, merely nestles in dead leaves, which hide it so perfectly that its large dark eyes are all that may be seen.

The depth and adornment of the scrape varies from species to species. In most plovers, the scrape is scarcely discernible, as if the hen had been caught away from home and had laid her egg forthwith where fortune found her, but individuals may add a few sticks or pebbles and may camouflage the eggs with grass or straw: the nest of the killdeer may be quite conspicuous, at least to human beings. The black-necked stilt sometimes lines its scrape with mussel shells, and crude linings are added on occasion by the pectoral sandpiper and many others; the snipe and the wandering tattler may actually build nests which can be lifted off the ground. (Like perching, swimming-and-diving and other habits usually ascribed to particular species, the construction of a crude but serviceable nest is probably an occasional phenomenon in the majority of sand-pipers, though few are so flexible as the painted snipe of Africa and Australia, which builds an elaborate nest in wet terrains and none at all where the ground is dry.[18]) Most species that nest in grass are at pains to bend grasses over the nest, so that it is invisible from above; the marbled godwit, on the other hand, merely stamps the grass flat and sits down.

Primitive though it is, the lowly scrape is more advanced than the nest of the Egyptian plover or blackbacked courser, which, like the rep-tiles from which it sprang, buries its eggs for incubation in warm earth. (This is supposedly the crocodile bird of which Herodotus wrote, "For when the crocodile . . . opens its jaws, which it does most commonly to-wards the west, the Trochilus enters its mouth and swallows the leeches. . . ." It is true that this species hangs around crocodiles and picks insects off them, but whether or not it enters the mouth is still disputed.) The white-fronted and Kittlitz's sand plover of the Old World and also one species of Patagonian seed snipe kick sand or dirt over their eggs when quitting the nest—an action which may have originated in haste and clumsiness and been retained as a habit because so effective. The dirt may also protect the nest from direct exposure to the sun, which apparently is harmful to the eggs of the mountain plover[76] and perhaps others. The American oystercatcher often leaves its eggs exposed, although in the raw fogs of Labrador, according to Audubon's account of its former nesting there, it "was found sitting as closely as any other bird."

Despite the humble nature of the scrape, its location and consecration are not suffered to pass without a ceremony, noted particularly in plovers and curlews, in which the female, tail high in the classic position and scratching earth out toward the rear the while, responds to the addresses of the male by rotating on one spot as, grandly, he circles in. Whether she kicks and excavates in sexual abandon and later makes the most of her own diggings, or whether she scratches out her scrape in some dim instinct that, from the looks of things, it must soon come in handy, are questions as depressing as they are rewarding, concerning as they do the matter of degree to which female ardor is reflexive and unconscious. In certain species, such as the northern phalarope, the lesser yellowlegs and many of the ringed plovers, the male may be inspired by the feverish domesticity of his mate to dig a whole series of abortive scrapes or "cock nests" before his passion for construction ebbs away.

The lapwing has a related habit, with a few continental refinements. To attract the hen's attention to his work, the cock first throws his diggings back over his shoulder in a devil-may-care manner, following which he tilts forward to a rakish angle and backs toward her, the better to bedazzle her with the fine colors of his underparts; he maintains this posture while the female, in a weary way, makes a brief survey of his excavations.

For the hen of the northern phalarope, the choice of scrape may be quite accidental: as the pressure of the egg increases, she flies back and forth from her tundra pool, visiting one scrape after another, and in one of these, as in musical chairs, sits down suddenly and lays.

Depending on the species, the occupants of 80 to 93 percent of all wild-bird eggs fail to reach maturity, and many are killed before seeing the light of day. Though egg camouflage is certainly a factor in reducing mortalities, the actual shape and size of the eggs appears to be of minor consequence; bird-egg contours, in fact, are very variable, from elongate to almost round. But in shorebirds, for several reasons, the shape of the egg is crucial, in part because of its large size; the eggs are so out of proportion to these delicate creatures that it is hard to look at them without a wince. The reason is that the new-hatched young must be exceptionally advanced even for precocial birds (as opposed to altricial birds, such as the blind and helpless young of robins) if they are to strike out for Tierra del Fuego, say, but a few weeks after they are hatched.

Most shorebird eggs are pyriform in shape, so that the smaller ends meet neatly in the center of the nest like wedges of a pie; otherwise, the bird would not be broad enough to incubate its own clutch. The placement tolerances are so fine that killdeer arrange their eggs with the small ends not only centered but pointed down, in order to reduce the egg area; should this arrangement be disturbed, it is quickly readjusted. The pyriform egg shape lends itself to emergencies, since the egg cannot travel very far; unlike a chicken egg, which will roll some distance, the pyriform egg, much smaller at one end, can roll only in a tight circle, which accounts for its occurrence among such cliff-ledge-nesting shorebird relatives as the murres and guillemots.

Shorebirds will often roll an escaped egg back into its scrape, a solution rather unusual among ground birds, for most of which the egg is meaningless except in the context of the clutch. This is not to imply that shorebirds are familiar with or even partial to their own eggs: the ringed plover of the Old World prefers a bright white egg with large black dots to its own obscure brown-speckled product, and the Eurasian oystercatcher will speedily abandon its own egg for what is known to the behaviorists as a "superoptimal stimulus" or "supernormal releaser"[103]—a huge artificial egg which, paradoxically, drives the bird into a perfect frenzy of sitting still. (Response to superoptimal stimuli is not confined to the lower animals: brassière padding and artificial coloring in food are but two of the innumerable stimuli employed by American commerce to "release" enthusiasm in our citizenry.)

The eggs of *Archaeopteryx* and its descendants were probably white, like reptiles' eggs, and the eggs of most hole-nesters and certain other birds have remained so: the crab plover, an aberrant shorebird of the north and west coasts of the Indian Ocean, is the solitary hole-nester in the suborder *Charadrii,* and it lays a lone white egg. Some ground-nesting families also lay white eggs, but shorebirds have developed eggs with cryptic markings. That the eggs of the solitary sandpiper are camouflaged like those of its relatives suggests that *T. solitaria* in the not too distant past was a ground-nester, and that the fragility noted in its eggs is not the reason for but the consequence of its arboreal habit.

The ground color of shorebird eggs may vary from buff and water-green to red or purple, but almost all are blotched with earthy brown at the end which blends with the scrape surroundings and scratched elsewhere with random streaks and squiggles serving to break the eggish outline. Egg coloration is closely related to the habitat in which the egg finds itself: the pepper-and-salt eggs of the piping plover are perfectly suited to the white quartz-and-garnet sands of Sagaponack. Like all shorebirds, this plover is equipped with color glands, though precisely how these work is still not known. (A remarkable adaptation is seen in the yellow-wattled lapwing of Asia, which in one small region of its range where the soil is reddish has evolved a reddish egg, very different from the old mud-colored egg that suits it elsewhere.)

Shorebird eggs are very variable even within a single species: rarely does the knot lay two alike. Some eggs are very colorful, as in the pectoral sandpiper, and others are modestly turned out, as in the sanderling. That the latter is a plain-spoken little bird of dour habits and demeanor, while the pectoral is showy and eccentric, might suggest some correlation here between egg and outlook, but the western, Baird's and purple sandpipers, all of them staid in appearance, lay eggs of extreme beauty, while the red phalarope, perhaps the gaudiest of all North American shorebirds, lays an egg of sullen and indifferent aspect. The jaçana is a glossy bird and lays a glossy egg, but almost all its shorebird kin are satisfied with eggs only slightly glossy, and the Hudsonian godwit, a retiring sort, lays eggs which have no gloss at all. Glossy or not, most shorebird eggs are water-resistant, since the undersides, especially among the lowland nesters, are often submerged in marshy water. (Eggs will tolerate complete submersion only briefly, and the stilt and the avocet, should their nests be flooded, shore them up out of the water by jamming sticks, old tennis shoes or other handy flotsam underneath, an adaptation to their environment which eerily resembles true intelligence.)

Almost all shorebirds nesting in the far north lay four eggs, presumably because four, fitting compactly into the nest, are the maximum that can be incubated. Both golden and semipalmated plover will sometimes lay three eggs; and while three are occasionally found in the nests of other species, it may be that these eggs represent a second nesting after the first clutch has been destroyed. The five to seven eggs found still more rarely are thought to be evidence of a nest shared by two pairs. It now appears that the sanderling (and also Temminck's stint of Eurasia) may lay two separate clutches in rapid succession, one of which is brooded by the cock.[76]

Shorebirds of more southerly range often content themselves with three eggs, and sometimes the snowy and Wilson's plovers and the black oystercatcher lay but two (the last-mentioned species may lay any number from one to four, and a nest of five eggs laid by a single hen has been reported.[108]) Where conditions of life, including the risks of long migration, are less arduous, a smaller brood will apparently sustain the species: even those birds which lay four eggs in the northern part of their range may hold at three when nesting farther south. "It is assumed that the clutch-size of each species . . . has hereditary basis, and that the number of eggs involved is ultimately determined by natural selection."[48]

Most shorebirds are determinate layers: that is, the size of the clutch is stable and not adjustable in response to external conditions. The entire clutch may be replaced if it is destroyed quite early, although the ruddy turnstone, an exception, apparently refuses to repeat itself. But single eggs, if broken or lost, are not replaced as they are among the gallinaceous birds, at least until incubation is well underway; it is the systematic removal of her egg that keeps the domestic hen laying day after day.

Before replacing a nest, a shorebird may repeat many of the preliminaries, even the song and aerial acrobatics. This time-wasting automatism, seen often in nature when its remorseless schedule of events is interrupted, is an example of nonadaptive behavior; the shorebird species that learned to forego such repetition would gain a tremendous competitive advantage over its near relatives.

Bird eggs mostly drop at dawn, but in the Arctic, at least, shorebirds may lay at any hour of the day.[109] Until the clutch has been completed, the egg is left to its own devices, and there may be an interval of several days between the completion of the clutch and the start of the incubation. Eggs can withstand considerable cold, at least until incubation has begun, and shorebirds, which usually lay one egg per day on successive days (the last eggs may be slightly behind schedule, especially in foul weather), pay them no heed until the setting instinct takes over from the laying one. It is almost as if, with the fall of the last egg, the bird blinked and its mind clicked over, like a meter; in that instant it stops gadding and sits down. The delayed incubation encourages simultaneous hatching of the young, a distinct advantage in a dangerous environment in which chicks must be separated from the telltale eggshells as rapidly as possible.

In species with sexual dimorphism, incubation is usually performed by the drab partner; it is the male phalaropes and not the hens which develop brood patches—two lateral areas of bare spongy skin hot with large blood vessels. The parent rolls each egg periodically as chicken farmers do: the turning may keep the germinal disk from being injured by floating upward and adhering to the shell membrane.

Shorebirds draw grass stems through their bills or otherwise distract themselves while on the nest—the setting killdeer may bang pebbles against each other—but they are perpetually on guard. In species in which parents share the nesting duties, the relief of the setting bird is

performed with care, lest attention be drawn to the nest. The upland
sandpiper creeps low through the grass for quite some distance, both
coming and going, and the willet, once its mate has slipped safely onto
the eggs, flies off with a distracting cry to draw attention from the exchange. The black oystercatcher relieves its mate when the tide is
down,[108] so that the bird relieved can feed immediately and easily.
Oystercatchers are silent upon leaving the nest; they do not flush until
some distance away and do not circle back. Nevertheless, the nests are
easily found and the clutch is small. The vulnerability of its nest is the
chief frailty of the American oystercatcher, a wary bird which in the days
of shorebird gunning passed man's decoys by without a nod.

In the open colonies of the avocet discretion is superfluous.
Ordinarily the setting bird will go to meet its mate, to which it bows in a
ceremonious manner. But should it decline to be relieved, the mate may
cry out sharply and start shoving until, nought else availing, the setting
bird is shouldered off the nest.

The most delicate relief rituals are performed by the stone plovers, a
family represented in North America by the two-striped thick-knee of
tropical latitudes: In the European species, at least, one mate signifies its
wish to be relieved by whistling to the other, which upon its arrival is
presented with a small pebble. Should the pebble be rejected, it is placed
between the eggs like a reproach, whereupon the injured partner "rises,
bows, and hurries in a crouched position from the nest."[4]

ESKIMO CURLEW

SEMIPALMATED PLOVER

9

The false lapwynge, full of trecherye. . .

—*Chaucer,* A Parliament of Fowles

. . . And sometimes I'll get thee young scamels [bar-tailed godwits] from the rock. . . ."

—*Shakespeare,* The Tempest

THE BRONZE-WINGED JAÇANA of southeast Asia, it is said, will destroy both eggs and nest rather than tolerate a meddler in its abode,[35] but the wind birds of the West stop short of such drastic Oriental measures. The *Charadrii,* in fact, are celebrated for the greatest range of distraction displays in all the bird world, though their ways of avoiding detection of eggs or young do not all qualify as true distractions: the oystercatchers, as has been noted, merely steal away, while the long-billed and bristle-thighed curlews and the marbled godwit may sit mutely where they are, as if confident of divine intervention. The thick-knee at times permits itself to be picked up off the nest, while the dotterel will actually come and sit on eggs held in the hand.[4] (The foolishness of this species was recognized as early as the fifteenth century: John Skelton wrote of "The doterell that folyshe pek/And also the mad coote/With a bald face to toote.") The western sandpiper will crawl under a hat placed on its nest while the white-rumped sandpiper may attack the prying hand. Even if driven off its eggs, the white-rump will creep back onto them within moments, passing slyly between the legs of the intruder if necessary; an old-time photographer of eggs would often discover in his lens that the clutch had been covered up again while he busied himself beneath his hood. Once accustomed to human presence, the sanderling, too, is fearless and may look on with indifference even when its young are lifted from the nest.

While most small shorebirds practice the oystercatcher tactic known as "furtive abandonment" (the behaviorist's term for "sneaking off": the abandonment of the Baird's sandpiper is usually so discreet that the nesting bird may not be seen at all), certain tundra-nesters have replaced unequivocal flight with a true distraction habit called the "rodent run." The purple sandpiper, acknowledged master of the rodent-runners, jumps into view a few feet from the nest and zigzags away, low and humped over, wing tips drooped in a simulation of hind legs, feathers fluffed like fur and squeaking like a mammal.[29] There is even a fortuitous resemblance between the black dorsal stripe of a fleeing lemming and the black line which splits the white rumps of most *Calidris,* so that a very nice imitation of the lemming is achieved—or nice enough, at any rate, to distract an unwise owl or Arctic fox.

The flaw in the rodent-run performance is like the flaw in the precautions of the hog-nosed snake, which rolls over on its back and plays dead so persuasively that it may be slung over a fence rail, but when turned right side up flips smartly onto its back again: The rodent-runner, if not pursued, rushes back to the starting point and begins all over, whistling this time for attention. Having first announced itself by shrill and aggressive behavior, it strolls carelessly away, pecking idly here and there as it goes along.

The sanderling, like the Baird's sandpiper, rarely indulges in the rodent run. After making off to a prudent distance, it reveals itself by a concerted flapping and commotion, interspersed with the strange frog notes practiced by the male in times of courtship. The ruddy turnstone, being conspicuous, also leaves the nest long before an intruder can come near.

The flap, creep and croak of the sanderling is a crude parody of the injury-feigning, rodent run and threat which characterize the distraction display of most other shorebirds. Threat display is marked in the tattlers. The willet and both yellowlegs will "mob" an enemy in the manner of crows, shrieking and diving with such violence that one fears for the integrity of one's scalp; the willet's temperament is so well suited to this practice that it will often mob just for the sake of mobbing, whether or not it has been stimulated by intruders.[107] Colonial nesters such as the stilt and avocet, which cannot count on camouflage to protect their eggs and young, also resort to loud cumulative outrage to dissuade their enemies, and the whimbrel, aroused, will feign an attack on man. Long-billed curlews, in nesting time, attack hawks without hesitation, and whimbrels attack ravens, while knots and turnstones will collide repeatedly against a prowling jaeger until the jostled bird beats a retreat; a male black-bellied plover struck "a jaeger so hard that it reeled unsteadily in mid-air."[9] That tundra species often nest in groups, leaving empty habitat on all sides, suggests that these concentrations have survival value as a defense against marauding jaegers, which rival the Arctic fox as the worst enemy of the wind birds in the far north. (Gulls, with their addiction to the eggs and young of other families, are the greatest enemy of most shorebirds south of the tundra, and the avocet is said[4] to have a warning cry which it reserves for gulls alone.)

Shrieking and diving is also practiced by the piping plover, which may copy the tactics of its excitable associate the least tern, but the piping plover is a harmless little bird, and its belligerence is so airy and inaudible that a victim who was not alert would scarcely be aware of it at all.

In flashing wing and rufous rump, respectively, the willet and killdeer are credited with baring "threat colors": the idea is that the sudden change of pattern will startle and discourage aggressors. But perhaps these devices are only a part of their distraction display; the hen woodcock, for example, is thought to raise the white spots on her under-tail coverts and rectrices to lure prowlers off into the woodland gloom.[8] Both willet and killdeer are virtuosos of diversion, even among wind birds, and besides threat color and loud abuse, they share a technique of sitting close until the final second, then exploding upward into the face of the intruder.

The explosion tactic is also practiced by the white-rumped sandpiper, the mountain plover and the surfbird. The Alaskan breeding range of the surfbird is nearly identical with the range of the Dall mountain sheep, and the first nest ever found, in 1926, was within a foot of a main sheep trail, which meant that its haggard occupants were exploding almost constantly. Having exploded, however, the surfbird reverts almost indifferently to injury-feigning, after which it may present itself sheepishly at its nest, even though the victim of its wiles is still on hand.

The surfbird explodes regularly in the face of man, a tactic which, applied on a narrow mountain trail, might prove effective in the case of heart condition or insecure footing but in the end may do more harm than good. The difference between this species and the killdeer and mountain plover is that while the latter birds will explode in the faces of grazing animals—after fluttering at the nest to head them off—they rarely pinpoint the location of the nest for such enemies as dogs and man.[40] For predators, as opposed to grazers, they go straight into that best known of all distractions, injury-feigning; the marvelous imitation of a crippled bird, wing dragging, whistling piteously, will lure small boys and dogs far off the track. (A further refinement is credited to the killdeer: if approached by a man on horseback, it will first shriek and flutter to turn aside the horse, then proceed with the broken-wing display to confound the rider.[8])

Injury-feigning, which may include self-prostration, imitation of juveniles, incipient hysteria, false-brooding (settling on nonexistent nests: this is popular among the piping plovers of Sagaponack) and many other nuances, has reached its highest expression in the ringed plovers, among which the killdeer is the undisputed champion. But it is also practiced in one form or another by most shorebirds other than the tattlers, whose noisy temperament is almost exclusively devoted to abuse and threat. Experiments with the Eurasian oystercatcher and ringed plover have shown that, confronted with a stuffed interloper of their own species, they resort to distraction displays after threats and attack have left their tormentor unmoved.[95] The golden plover, avocet and black-necked stilt, all of which "demonstrate," are also experts at distraction: the stilt may hoist one wing in such a way that the wind twists and rumples it unmercifully, as if it were smashed, and its manner of collapsing one leg will bring all right-thinking predators on the dead run.

The renowned sagacity of fox and weasel has proved no match for the distraction displays staged for their benefit by the knot. The imperiled mountain plover seems to go into convulsions, while the Wilson's plover lies down on the ground and "gasps," as if about to breathe its last. The hen dunlin has become so upset by an imitation of the call-note of her young that she "literally rolled about on the ground with feathers ruffled; it was quite impossible to see her head or beak emerging from the disheveled bundle. . . ."[8] Most spectacular of all are the communal distractions of the pratincoles, which litter the earth with individuals in all stages of decrepitude, and of the pied stilt of New Zealand, which may quite suddenly collapse and "die" in groups of five or six.

All of these displays suggest that injury-feigning is a happy accident born of ineffective threat, and perhaps related to—though not the same as—displacement activities, which have been defined as "either a haphazard set of distorted actions reflecting a lack of muscular coordination and nervous control, or . . . the substitution of an existing stereotyped pattern from an entirely different context in the bird's repertoire, usually in consequence of two conflicting 'emotional' drives which inhibit expression of each."[29] In other words, what was originally a kinesis, or helpless thrashing—in effect, a vain attempt to flee and attack at the same time—proved so distracting to the predator that a sort of "nervous breakdown" became a fixed, heritable habit of defense.

Injury-feigning in the spotted sandpiper is most intense about five days before the eggs hatch out, subsiding gradually as the young begin to grow. The incubation of the shorebirds is relatively brief, lasting ordinarily from 21 to 24 days; the semipalmated sandpiper, markedly faster, hatches at 17 to 19 days.[74] Its dispatch in the vulnerable nesting period may partly account for the prosperity of the species, which is among the most common shorebirds in North America.

A century ago, the golden plover was probably the most abundant of the wind birds, closely followed by the Eskimo curlew. At present, the most numerous are those small sandpipers which were relatively unmolested by the gunners until the flocks of larger birds gave out. The semipalmated sandpiper, which was recorded[6] in May of 1964 at Kitts Hummock, Delaware, in a flock estimated at 75,000, is the likely champion, but the least sandpiper and sanderling are also prolific little birds. So is the northern phalarope, which occurs in every ocean and has been seen in flotillas of many thousands in the Humboldt Current and elsewhere: its abundance is fortunate, for this phalarope is so tame that it is hunted commonly and with great success by very young Eskimo children. But if world populations are considered, the dunlin may be the most numerous shorebird on earth: it is a common species on this continent, and is much the most numerous sandpiper of Europe.[40]

The hatching of the chicks, which usually peck their way out of their shells within a few hours of one another, is a crucial time for the shorebirds in the contest for survival. As soon as possible, the parent sanderling removes the empty shells, the pale interiors of which are quickly spotted by the hawking jaegers. Sometimes the adult assists the hatching by removing the egg cap as the chick pecks itself free;[75] the stone curlew may wrench off the cap, help free the chick, then carry off, stamp on and consume the pieces. The spotted sandpiper may also eat part of the shell, while the lapwing resolves the problem by tucking the bits of shell under its nest.[66] Eggshell removal may be related to nest sanitation, since the fecal sacs of the chicks are also removed, and doubtless the broken fragments would irritate the adult's brood patch as well as the new skins of the young, but whatever its origin, the trait has great survival value. Even the avocet, a colonial nester, will sometimes carry off its shells and those of its neighbors as well, depositing them in the nearest water. In the woods, eggshell removal may be less urgent, to judge from the behavior of a woodcock that ignored the eggshells throughout the hatching period.[76] The common snipe, which hides its nest under bent grasses, appears to omit the practice entirely.[66]

Much egg yolk remains in the stomach of the chick to tide it over its first hours. This is important in bad weather, for exposure to cold rains of the arctic summer will kill a chick in a short time; should bad weather persist, the chick may starve to death while keeping warm. But most shorebird young, after drying for an hour or so in wind and sun, take to life straightaway (the thick-knee, which is semiprecocial, is the North American exception), leaving the nest permanently within the first 24 hours (both golden and black-bellied plover may remain a few hours longer). For this reason, precocial birds are known as "nidifuges" or "nest fugitives." It is questionable how far the nest fugitives go; a pair of spotted sandpipers stayed within 50 yards of their nest site for 19 days after the chicks hatched,[47] and in the piping plover, the chicks usually remain within 500 feet of home during the 30 to 35 days before they are fledged, despite the stretches of open beach on every side.[111] Probably this area is an approximation of the breeding territory of the parents, although this species will cross territorial lines to help herd the chicks of neighbors out of harm's way.

Some nest fugitives are a bit slow getting started. The black-necked stilt, with its long legs, wobbles like a colt for a day or more, and the black oystercatcher must be brooded for about 36 hours after hatching; sometimes, young oystercatchers of both species are fed by their parents for several days. The adults bring food and, dropping it off before the young, "point to it with their great red bills."[68] Snipe and woodcock also bring food to their young and probably feed them. Chicks of some species are led to food and instructed in its use through demonstration, while others, though tended by adults, feed from the start by trial and error: a sanderling brood, upon leaving the nest, "probed about, investigating everything they encountered. The oldest tested a purple saxifrage petal and swallowed plant bits."[75] The chicks learn quickly all that their parents can teach them, but the young oystercatcher lives several months before it can deal efficiently with bivalves, barnacles, chitons, limpets and other such grudging fare.

The banded stilt nests along salt lakes of interior Australia; its eggs are salt-white, and so are its downy young. Chicks of the piping plover, like their eggs, are salt-and-peppered, to match their dune surroundings, while chicks of most other species have broken color patterns on the back and head appropriate to their habitat. These patterns so fragment the puffball bodies that, pressed to the ground, they have no more substance than blown flower silk.

Sanderling chicks are apt to walk about while the parents are off feeding, but like most chicks, will hide or freeze at an alarm note from the parent and are drawn forth again by softer whistles. In the spotted sandpiper, the male puffs out his feathers like a setting hen, in signal to the chicks that they may now rejoin him; the avocet uses this "false-brooding" position to draw chicks away from a place of danger. But often the chicks are so well hidden that their parents may have difficulty reassembling them, to judge from the fact that many are fitted out with special white wing feathers or other recognition marks: when scattered or otherwise separated from the parent, they raise white wings like tiny flags.[109] Although generally more silent than tree- or hole-nesting young, they now emit thin ventriloquial peeps—sounds so wispy and diminutive that the listener cannot tell where they are coming from or say for sure that he heard anything at all. Presumably this talent for ventriloquism, shared by most shorebird young, is an adaptation which confuses would-be predators while permitting the parent to locate its scattered brood.

Until they are fledged, the chicks depend on their parents for protection; a piping plover may knock a chick flat if it does not freeze promptly at the warning signal.[111] Repeatedly, in the average day, the chicks must crouch upon the ground and maintain strict motionless silence until another whistle tells them all is well. (Young reptiles and squid will also crouch in the same manner,[85] though doubtless these creatures would fail to respond to whistling of any kind.) Relative silence is characteristic of the young of open-nesters, and response to warning signals so innate that the peeping chick of grouse and many other birds falls silent at a signal from the parent even before it hatches from the egg.

In the eighth hour of its life, a semipalmated plover has been seen to catch and eat an insect, and a piping plover can run short distances at a speed exceeding four miles per hour when but two days old. The extreme precocity in shorebird chicks has been well demonstrated in experiments[68] with new-hatched killdeer and spotted sandpipers. The killdeer opened its eyes and called when 2 minutes old, sat up at 9 minutes, pecked at a spot and walked about on its tarsi toward the end of the first hour, was briefly on its feet at 66 minutes, held its wings straight out 16 minutes later, was walking at 1½ hours; it ran 7 inches, drank a drop of water, preened and fell down flat before it was 2 hours old. At the start of its third hour, it ate fish.

Similarly, the spotted sandpiper achieved full teeter at 31 minutes and was quick on its feet in its tenth hour. Incidental observations added the following to the natural histories of these species: In its first days, the killdeer (which afterward took up for good the indirect or over-the-wing head-scratching of all plovers, oystercatchers, stilts and avocets) scratched its head from beneath its wing. And a young spotted sandpiper, given a choice, disdained insects in favor of custard.

The behaviorist must distinguish between innate, heritable behavior, such as the foot-patting observed in a woodcock chick raised separately from its parents, and behavior, such as the young oystercatcher's mastery of its bill, which may be based, in part, on imitation. The short-billed dowitcher and the stilt sandpiper, which associate in migration (their tundra habitats are quite different), have developed what appears to be an imitative or behavioral convergence:[8] both tend to feed belly-deep in water, both feed in close methodical groups and both have evolved varieties of the same whistled *wheu*, which they share with their associate, the lesser yellowlegs.

A more striking example of convergent behavior is the ploverlike attitudes of the upland and buff-breasted sandpipers, which have short plover bills and plover feeding traits, prefer the sedate company of plovers to that of their own family and even scatter upon alighting the way plovers do; the first-named bird is still called commonly the "upland plover."

The solitary and spotted sandpipers and the wandering tattler share a

quite similar ringing call when flushed as well as the most pronounced
teeter actions among all North American shorebirds; the tattler and spotted sandpiper, as already noted, also share a curious shallow wingbeat to
transport themselves short distances. (This wingbeat is reflected in the
courtship flight of many species which do not resort to it at other times.)
Yet all three are nonflocking species which rarely associate with one another; in this case, instinctive behavior inherited from a common ancestor can probably be assumed.

Instinct, a term used so indiscriminately that some authorities would
like to abandon it altogether, has been defined as "an inborn, particulate,
stereotyped form of co-ordinated behavior characteristic of a given animal species."[109] Instinctive behavior does not necessarily benefit the
behaver: the tendency in the black oystercatcher chick to hide its head
when alarmed,[8] seems decidedly nonadaptive. And the unbending nature of its instinct may lead the shorebird to predicament or worse; this
is manifest in nearly all areas of bird behavior. The greater yellowlegs,
yelping wildly at man's approach, has been named among the wariest of
shorebirds, yet there is a drastic limitation to its prudence. "It would
seem almost as though these birds drew an abstract danger line, difficult
to cross from the outside without alarming them, but once inside which,
man became to them a mere harmless item of the landscape."[8]

Certain shorebirds are credited with an example of adaptive behavior
that would do credit to far more intelligent creatures: oystercatchers[35]
and thick-knees are said to move their eggs to a new site if an old one
proves precarious or otherwise unsatisfactory, and the woodcock, willet
and spotted sandpiper, more astonishingly still, have all been reported to
carry their young between their legs from scenes of danger. These reports
are so numerous that one must repress an impulse to dismiss them out of
hand; it is conceivable, at least, that chicks are sometimes caught up accidentally on the feet of close-setting species as the bird flies from the nest.
And a friend of mine has filmed an African jaçana as it made off with its
newly hatched chick under its wing.

Shorebird chicks, running here and there through sedge and tussock,
learn to follow their own parents by means of a process known as im-

printing. After its first hours, the chick will become afraid of moving objects larger than itself, but before this happens, it has placed its faith in its parents. Given its head, it would as soon tag after a passing fox or a rubber duck pulled by a string, whichever happened along first, and in later life—since these familial responses are related—would theoretically seek out a fox or a rubber duck for its own mate. Imprinting was thought at first to be irreversible,[51] and it is true that a Eurasian oyster-catcher became permanently addicted to the silkie fowl which were its foster parents. But it is now thought that some species, if not all, may forget the imprinter over a period of time if the latter fails to put in an appearance. Shorebirds, in any case, are less attracted to false parents than are ducks or fowl: "Especially curlews (*Numenius arquata*), even when hatched artificially and never having seen any living creature but their keeper, cannot be brought to respond to him with any reactions but those of escape."[51]

Young avocets, like the young of gulls and man, may loiter about in gangs. As in these other colonial animals, one of the gang is sometimes singled out for severe attack by a parent of another: this usually incites a general squabble which can degenerate into a free-for-all in which the youthful victim may be sorely trampled.[105]

In many shorebirds, the downy young are guided by the male until they are fledged, which usually occurs by the end of their first three weeks; the semipalmated sandpiper may y after 14 days. In the snipe, whimbrel, Hudsonian godwit and golden plover, the brood is divided between the parents and reared in two separate detachments. Some chicks are abandoned before they can fly, but the male ruddy turnstone will escort his chicks for a week or more after they are fledged. Still, the turnstone will start southward well before his young and is rare on the breeding grounds after the end of July.

The southbound turnstone will be considerably behind the cock of the pectoral sandpiper which, far from escorting its chicks until after they are fledged, abandons the breeding grounds soon after it has mated. Its departure appears to coincide with the decline of the fly-larvae cycle, early in July, and since it is one of the commonest species on the arctic slope (the pectoral nests from sea level to 1,200 feet), there is a theory[84] that its desertion is no feckless thing but an adaptive trait which lessens competition for the food supply. It seems as likely, however, in view of the great food abundance of the North, that the male pectoral simply leads a life apart, as does the ruff.

The early departure of shorebird adults may replace intolerance toward juveniles (witnessed in blue geese,[17] bears and other creatures) as an encouragement to dispersal and a defense against inbreeding: it is very unlikely that the southbound young ever alight at the same destination as their parents. The staggered departure also serves to lessen competition on the feeding grounds of the migration route, where the adults would tend to be more aggressive and efficient than their young.

Those young that survive the first year of their life—and they are not many—may live for a long time as birds go, matching a growing store of experience and dim knowledge against the onset of senility. In North America, a banded piping plover 14 years old is the longest-lived wild shorebird recorded, but a Eurasian curlew, *N. arquata* (this species is the Old World counterpart of the long-billed curlew, in the same way that the little curlew and Eskimo curlew are counterparts), banded in Sweden on July 4, 1926, was still in "perfect condition" when shot in January of 1958 at Norfolk, England, and a banded Eurasian oystercatcher attained the age of 34. (The age and condition of the curlew suggests the gloomy possibility that in the Texas sightings of the Eskimo curlew from 1945 through the spring of 1963, the same few birds may have been seen, year after year.)

Few wild creatures perish of old age. Sooner or later, in the wild, some combination of inherent weakness, injury, disease, parasites or competition, or migration barriers, or inclement season—for example, long days of cold November rain which leach away the feather oils and insulation—will cause the wind bird to fall to the hawk or storm that in its years of strength it had outflown.

BLACK-BELLIED PLOVER

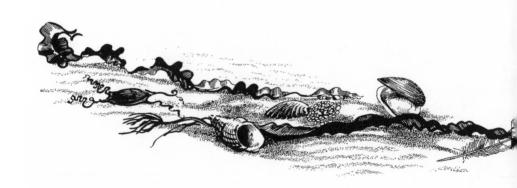

BLACK-BELLIED PLOVER

10

The little flock [sanderlings] wheeled out over the bay in a wide circle,
flashing white wing bars; they returned, crying loudly as they passed over
the flats where the young were still running and probing at the edge of the
curling wavelets; they turned their heads to the south and were gone.
                    —*Rachel Carson,* Under the Sea Wind

PREPARATIONS for long-distance flight demand a great part of
the wind bird's year, and birds nesting on Alaska's northern
coasts begin to form migration flocks as early as late June.
Unlike certain ducks, shorebirds are not flightless during their
postnuptial molt, and wing molt in particular may be delayed until the
bird's arrival on its winter grounds.

By mid-August, in the Arctic, even the young of many species have
already gone. Scattered birds range wistfully across the tundra, as if in
search of the vanished horde, or gather in small restless bands on the
coastal flats. But at Nunivak Island in the Bering Sea, in the last week of
August 1964, ruddy turnstones, red and northern phalaropes, dunlin,

western and rock sandpipers and wandering tattlers were still common; individual birds must have lingered on into September. Snow comes to the subarctic in September, and most migrants will leave before the snows, which blur the landmarks on which birds depend in distance travel. The dunlin, however, may wait for the first white days before departing.

When the last dunlin leaves the Colville Delta on the Arctic Sea, the pectoral sandpiper which puffed and boomed on the far side of its sedgy pool may be settled for the winter in the Argentine. Leaving the Arctic, as it often does, by the end of June, the pectoral alights in Manitoba in early July, in South Carolina two weeks later, in Barbados by mid-August and in the Argentine at the month's end. Unlike most shorebirds, the pectoral makes haste on its southward as well as on its northward journey, and the juveniles are not far behind: some of the pectorals arriving on the pampas toward the end of August, after a journey of 7,000 miles, are still weak and immature, with yellow natal down still on the head.[45]

> The potential energy stored up in the small richly colored eggs of this northern sandpiper is almost beyond comprehension. The downy chicks, as soon as they are out of the shell, show wonderful activity. . . . They know at birth how to hide among the hummocks and vegetation so as to defy the sharpest eyes. In three weeks they are awing and six weeks later they are off on their long journey to the south, crossing mighty mountain ridges, great stretches of land and of sea.[10]

The queer behavior of the pectoral sandpiper does not cease with its retirement from the breeding grounds. Perhaps it departs with its instincts unfulfilled, for one male in three may set up and defend territories wherever it stops on its route southward, despite the absence of female inspiration. The territory can be as small as 4 square yards or as large as 44 square yards, and this area is hotly defended, not only against other pectorals, but against trespassing lesser yellowlegs and semipalmated and least sandpipers (the leasts, however, are ignored in late July, when the pectorals' belligerence begins to wane). Killdeer and solitary sandpipers, on the other hand, do not seem to antagonize the pectoral, and may wander its kingdoms as they please.[41]

Skirmishes traditionally take place at borders, and so it is among the pectorals. The skirmishes are characterized by the "wing-away" threat display so pervasive among *Calidris*, in which the wing on the side away from the aggressor is lifted in the air; by mock feeding (the defender may jab smartly at the ground as the aggressor nears) or mock fighting; by nervous defecation; and, uncommonly, by actual combat.

After a fight, the loser usually flies off, but sometimes it simply crouches before its opponent, which may or may not kick, peck and trample it into the mud. (In the Arctic, at least, sparring pectorals emit harsh sounds both "flatulent and loud."[84]) Afterward, both loser and victor may displacement-feed while they compose themselves, shaking their feathers back in place, whereupon the loser, on an impulse one can appreciate if not applaud, may turn on a small and inoffensive neighbor and attack it without provocation. This reaction is known to the behaviorists as "redirection activity." At the end of the day, the pectoral rejoins the other shorebirds. Forced by darkness to abandon its game, it permits the flocking instinct to triumph over its misanthropy until the dawn.

It is not known whether migrant territoriality is anachronistic and nonadaptive, or whether the resultant dispersion of the birds contributes to full utilization of the food supply, and even to the prevention of epidemic. Algal poisoning is common among birds which feed in the stagnant shallows of late summer, and the competition among migrating male pectorals may help to explain a strange and morbid scene witnessed[41] occasionally at this season: A pectoral stricken with botulism or other ailment and flopping out its life upon the flat may be surrounded by a circle of other pectorals which do not seem to wish it well. The onlookers are stiff and taut, as if prepared to intervene should the ailing bird attempt to regain its feet.

The pectoral sandpiper is not alone in its postnuptial belligerence; it is only exceptionally intense. The lesser yellowlegs, sanderling and semi-palmated sandpiper, among others, display symptoms of the amatory instinct when they return to Sagaponack in July, and the last species in particular stages small cockfights all over the expanses of the sandy gut. (The thick-knees of Europe hold communal dances in autumn, a custom apparently unrelated to sexual recrudescence.)

Species that winter in the Northern Hemisphere may require several months to pass southward through a given spot: southbound black-bellied plovers and semipalmated sandpipers, for example, are regularly at Sagaponack from July into November, and a few are still present at Christmas. But individual birds rarely tarry very long, and when the day comes to move on, they travel rapidly: a banded ruddy turnstone has been known to journey over 450 miles in a single day, and a banded lesser yellowlegs averaged 385 miles per day in a journey from Cape Cod to Martinique.[112]

The sanderlings, joining the scattered members of their kind which have summered in the salt haze of our outer beaches, are not the first wind birds to appear. Short-billed dowitchers, lesser yellowlegs and semipalmated and least sandpipers, all of which may nest as far south as middle Canada, precede them by several days; the lesser yellowlegs occasionally returns before the end of June. At Sagaponack, in the year that I kept a record, the least sandpipers appeared first, on July 6, followed within the week by semipalmated sandpipers, lesser yellowlegs, whimbrel, a pectoral sandpiper and dowitchers, in that order (piping plover and a pair of spotted sandpipers were in residence); these birds were joined before the month was out by killdeer, greater yellowlegs, a few knot and black-bellied plover, a western sandpiper and a stilt sandpiper.

By early August, most of the first wave was gone. In late August and early September came a second major wave of black-bellied, golden and semipalmated plover, dunlin, western sandpipers and a white-rumped sandpiper, together with birds of the year in their juvenal plumage and some laggard pectorals. Probably this wave included some non-breeding wanderers. It is the latter group that often includes the accidental birds out of the Old World, since young birds are those most apt to stray. I search the dunlin flocks each year for the curlew sandpiper of Eurasia (which has been recorded once at Sagaponack), but so far I have had to be content with a lone bird seen years ago in Africa.

When Indian summer is still bright and warm, most of the piping plover will be gone from the Sagaponack outer beach.

> Early departure from its nesting ground is not imperative in the case of the southerly breeding bird, but the habit is undoubtedly of long stand-ing and dates back to the time when the species bred close to the edge of the glacial ice fields and summer passed quickly.[8]

Assuming this supposition to be correct, one wonders if the piping plover was not originally a population of semipalmated plover that failed to follow the glacier's retreat back toward the Arctic and evolved sepa-rately through partial isolation, like the pale killdeer of the Caribbean.

Migrant shorebirds consort in a large flock composed of species flocks—not a common habit among birds—and the open nature of their habitats helps in making observation simple, though identification may be quite another matter: the small sandpipers, or peep, rank with terns (*Sterna*), the small sparrows, *Empidonax* flycatchers and fall warblers as the nemesis of the beginner. The problem of identifying peep is com-pounded in the summer and fall by molts and transitional plumages, which may assert themselves in such disorder that no two birds in ten of the same species look alike. Sanderlings and semipalmated sandpipers are the worst culprits in this respect and may range in August from spring red to winter gray, with myriad scraggy intermediates.

> The most elementary knowledge of shorebird plumages appears to serve the purpose of many field observers. But often there is that bird in the flock—or an entire flock—that doesn't fit the picture in some familiar book, or wears a "wrong" plumage for the season, and so on. The changes might be likened to a problem in relative motion—time and rate that feathering is acquired or lost, and interval it may be retained, vary. Two, or even three, generations of feathers (plumages) may be more or less pre-sent, each on its own schedule. Other variables include species differences, age, sex, sometimes color phases, and effect of wear and fading.[73]

Because the close similarity of their habitats has led to a general conformism, the field marks of the peep tend to be relative and not helpful
except in the most classic individuals. Despite the variety of characters
and habits attributed to it, the most difficult of all peep to identify is
probably the Baird's sandpiper, especially where, as in Sagaponack, one is
so rarely exposed to it; it sometimes seems that the only way to identify a
suspect is to eliminate, step by step, the possibility that it might be
something else. This is a negative and somehow unsatisfactory method,
and while I have used it to pin down two Baird's sandpipers over the
years, I went home entirely satisfied with neither one.

In its rarity at Sagaponack (it is a rare bird anywhere on the Atlantic
coast), the Baird's sandpiper is an exception. To the margins and vicinity
of Sagaponack Pond come more than half of the shorebird species of
North America, not only because of the pond's location on the Atlantic
flyway but because of the range of habitats in a small area. At the eastward end, the ocean beach and brackish pond margin, mud and saw
grass and rank meadow are all within a hundred yards of one another;
killdeer and golden plover visit the potato fields behind the pond, and
not far inland, in the swamp that lies between Sagaponack and
Poxabogue, the haunts of the woodcock and solitary sandpiper begin.

While it is true that certain species rarely stray to the salt water and
that others rarely leave it, most shorebirds cross habitat lines more or less
freely, and some of the more successful species, such as the black-bellied
plover and the killdeer, the spotted sandpiper and both yellowlegs, may
be seen in a variety of habitats, depending upon local opportunity.

In fact, the habitats assigned to many shorebirds are so arbitrary as to
be of little value. Of the Wilson's phalarope, Wilson's plover, buff-
breasted sandpiper, long-billed dowitcher and Hudsonian godwit, each
of which I have seen at Sagaponack once, only the godwit was where one
might have thought to look. The Wilson's phalarope, in the eight days of
its stay, was never seen to go anywhere near the water (this species is the
least aquatic of the phalaropes); it tiptoed endlessly up and down on the
dry flats, its needle bill dabbing tiny midges faster than two per second.
The long-billed dowitcher, which is thought to prefer fresh water, stayed

at the salt end of the pond, just inside the ocean beach, while the flock of nine buff-breasted sandpipers, more at home in the meadows and cultivated fields which surround the pond, wandered tamely on a tide flat of the opened gut, in full sight and hearing of the surf. (George Mackay, whose game lists include owls and vultures, could not bring himself to shoot this confiding bird on the one occasion that it presented itself among his decoys, but Western sportsmen were unmoved; in the hunting years, the buff-breasted sandpiper was decimated or worse. Even after all its mates had been shot down, it would call out hopefully to the decoys, much preferring wooden company to none at all.)

In the late summer of 1960, when the buff-breasts came, a hurricane had caused the surf to breach the dunes, and the sea took the whole pond with it when it washed out again. The exposed flats, all that September, were overrun with birds, and one soft gleaming morning, these fragile bits of silver and pale gold appeared out of the sky to join the rest. They walked about in the way often ascribed to them—lifting their feet, that is, as if stepping over and through the grass they are accustomed to, and craning their heads as if to peer over impediments which on the open flats do not exist. With their round eyes and tentative manner, the nine seemed astonished to find themselves so far off course: "So this is the sea!" their expressions seemed to say. The next day they were gone.

The Wilson's plover, attended by a solitary sandpiper and a semipalmated plover, bobbed and preened on the mud hummocks of Little Poxabogue, a shallow slough of lily pads and painted turtles closely set about with woods, three miles inland. It was early September, a red bright day of Indian summer sun and stillness, and the beach bird stood immobile for a time, observing the turtles and a muskrat, two black ducks and a green heron, as if certain of its central place in a strange and beautiful new universe.

WHIMORET

II

Voices of plover.
I stare
Into the darkness of the star-lit promontory.
                                    —Bashō (Seventeenth century)
Through throats where many rivers meet, the curlews cry,
Under the conceiving moon, on the high chalk hill. . . .
                    —Dylan Thomas, "In the White Giant's Thigh"

MOST SHOREBIRDS leave the breeding grounds before the adverse days round to the fore, and those that do not are rarely driven southward by cold weather. Surfbirds, rock sandpipers and black turnstones, waiting for low tides at Wrangell Inlet, keep company all winter on the docks and warehouse roofs of Petersburg, Alaska;[34] other surfbirds winter on hot tropic coasts. So long as there is food, in other words, a remarkable range of temperature can be sustained, and food may still be plentiful when the

wind birds rise from the moon rim of the northern waters and fly toward the southern stars. While not as strong as the spring impulse, the
migratory urge of fall causes several species to leave behind the rich
crowberry crops and intertidal zones of the maritime North Atlantic
summer for the high winds and hungry sea of a long transoceanic
crossing.

Favorable winds are less crucial than was once assumed. A gale may
discourage the flocks from setting out, but once the migrants are aloft
and underway, streaming across the stars of wild night skies, they will fly
into the teeth of adverse winds. There is much evidence that strong
winds are preferred to windlessness, providing the lift that carries the
birds for hours over land and sea.

The frequency with which the wind birds rest at sea is still debated.
While many species have been seen to alight and swim on sheltered water, good sight records of shorebirds alighted on the ocean—always ex-
cepting the red and northern phalaropes—are virtually nonexistent.
Nevertheless, in May of 1907, an experienced naturalist[38] saw a migration of "near a thousand" willets resting on the open sea of the Grand
Banks; since the birds were so close that they had to flutter up from the
path of the ship, it is hard to believe that this well-marked species could
have been mistaken for anything else. (The size of the willet flock and its
location southeast of Newfoundland is almost as astonishing as the mass
settlement upon the sea; that the flock had gone astray in fog and passed
east of a destination in Nova Scotia is my own unsatisfactory explanation.)

Present opinion is that while many species can and will rest on the
surface if necessary, they do not often do so out of choice, nor can they
survive long if the sea is rough. (Whales and sea turtles, before their great
numbers were reduced by commercial slaughter, may have provided resting points throughout the tropic seas; the red phalarope, at least, has
been seen to use both animals in this manner.[72]) Thus the gale winds
that sometimes carry shorebirds far off course and scatter the immature
and inexperienced to strange coasts must also drown them in considerable numbers. Winds have carried ocean birds so far inland and south-

bound birds so far into the north that, tired and disoriented, the impulse toward migration spent, they linger where they find themselves: in a great storm of November 1888 this fate befell large flocks of killdeer, few of which managed to survive the long Massachusetts winter.

But true invasions—in which meaningful numbers of a certain species, strayed or storm-borne, establish a breeding population far beyond their usual range—are very rare: the only bird species which have invaded the North American land mass within the memory of man are the fieldfare, a European thrush blown to Greenland in a 1937 storm and now resident at the island's southwestern tip, and the cattle egret, an Afro-Asian species which, after millennia in its natural range, now seems intent on populating the whole world.

Among shorebirds, the closet thing to a North American invasion occurred in 1927. Large flocks of lapwings known to have left England for Ireland on the night of December 18-19 were overtaken by fog and violent winds, and by December 20 appeared in thousands throughout the Maritime Provinces of Canada, from Baffin Island to New Brunswick.[86] Had they arrived at a benign time of year, a few might have established themselves, but in a very few days the last of them died of cold and hunger. A few greater golden plover turn up in late May every year near Stephenville Crossing, Newfoundland,[74] but where they nest—their nearest known breeding ground is Iceland—remains a mystery.

Ruffs and curlew sandpipers appear regularly on our North Atlantic coast (the first ruff was recorded before the Civil War, on Long Island; since then it has turned up at least once in every state from Maine to North Carolina), although the prevailing winds are set against them; redshanks and other European birds come also. But the obstacles against westward wandering across the Atlantic are great, and it may be that some of the accidental visitors do not come direct from Europe but from southward points on their migration route, riding the east winds of the Canary Current or the tropical storms that build off the coast of Africa. This possibility might help explain why that great wanderer, the curlew sandpiper, which breeds in central and eastern Siberia (a first North American nesting was reported in 1962, from the vicinity of Point

Barrow[11]) but winters as far west as Africa, turns up not on the Pacific coast, as one might expect, but on the Atlantic seaboard. It is also possible "that a few individuals may migrate in fall from their Siberian nesting grounds east by way of Alaska and Canada to the Atlantic seaboard—a route used by certain shorebirds breeding in tundra country. . . ."[11]

North American birds, conversely, have no trouble getting lost, riding rapidly to Europe on the strong westerlies of the North Atlantic; the jet streams of high altitudes would blow them there in a matter of hours. New World visitors, especially in Great Britain, are comparatively abundant (bird-watchers are also abundant in Britain, but this does not entirely account for the high incidence of accidentals), and the most frequent visitors by far are the *Charadrii*. Yellowlegs of both species go regularly to Europe, as do the long-billed dowitcher and solitary sandpiper. But the commonest wanderer, with 62 recorded sightings, is the pectoral sandpiper, which goes too far in so many other directions as well.

A more surprising chronic stray is the buff-breasted sandpiper. Like the stilt sandpiper, the buff-breast has very narrow migration lanes, clinging close to the 100th meridian, and it ventures even more rarely than its kinsman as far east as the Atlantic coast: in the spring, it is so faithful to its route that the majority of buff-breast migrants cross the Gulf of Mexico[112,53] and alight in certain fields near Rockport, Texas, then make a second long-distance flight to certain fields near Edmonton, Alberta, being very uncommon at other likely places in between. But while the prudent stilt sandpiper has remained a homebody, daring but one recorded visit across the Atlantic,[40] the far-flung buff-breast of the fall has delighted and surprised new friends not only in England but in France, Switzerland, Helgoland and Egypt; it has been said[70] that the autumn buff-breast is more likely to turn up in England than in "any area of similar size in eastern North America."

Other anomalies have been noted[70] among transatlantic vagrants. Species common on the coast (*cf.* semipalmated sandpiper) and also those which make long transoceanic migrations (*cf.* golden plover) cross the Atlantic far *less* often than several species of more inland distribution (buff-breasted and upland sandpipers), whereas species which breed in the western Nearctic (*cf.* long-billed dowitcher) wander *more* commonly to Europe than those breeding farther east (*cf.* short-billed dowitcher): the pectoral sandpiper of Siberia and Alaska is eight times as common in England as the Baird's sandpiper, even though the Baird's nests as close as Greenland. The theory is that the western nesters, which mainly strike eastward before heading south, are more apt to carry on to England than species which set out on a more southerly course at the beginning of migration; the same tendency, in reverse, may in part account for the 1927 invasion of lapwings, populations of which migrate west to Ireland in the autumn. (Spring records in Britain of the buff-breasted and Baird's sandpipers and the northern phalarope, which in this season are extremely rare on the Atlantic coast of North America, may represent individuals which strayed from South America to Africa, then proceeded north. The killdeer, unlike all other species, visits Britain most commonly in *winter,* perhaps in consequence of its luckless habit of being blown back north by winter storms.)

Shorebird wanderers have not been limited to European travel. The Hudsonian godwit has flown at least 12 times to New Zealand, a place so removed from its natural haunts that one must suppose that it followed the bar-tailed godwits which belong there. (The Hudsonian godwit and several other North American shorebirds recorded in New Zealand have never been recorded in Australia, but a few hundred miles away;[27] whether this is a tribute to the bird watchers of New Zealand or a phenomenon of zoogeography is not yet known.) In 1953, the sharp-tailed sandpiper of Siberia, which occurs in migration in northwest Alaska and winters in the southwest Pacific, turned up at Tristan da Cunha,[27] a small volcanic peak of a submerged mountain range in the Atlantic wastes between Africa and South America. The red phalarope has found itself as far inland as Kansas and Colorado, while a jaçana has alighted on a ship 40 miles at sea, off the coast of Surinam.[92] Young long-billed dowitchers, Wilson's phalaropes and western willets straggle eastward in late summer as far as the Atlantic seaboard (fall willets at Sagaponack are more likely to be westerns than not), a form of juvenile wandering analogous to the northward explorations of young summer egrets. Post-juvenile dispersion, as it is called, cannot be accounted for on the basis of food alone; in many creatures besides man, the young are more adventurous and less set in their ways, and thus prone to disorganized behavior.

The westerly winds of the northern land mass that account for a general west-east drift of autumn migrants may also explain this curious characteristic of shorebird distribution—that almost none of them winter west or even southwest of their breeding grounds.[27] Even those long-billed dowitchers and pectoral sandpipers that breed in Siberia return east to North America before migrating southward, and the European ringed plover that breeds in Baffin Island goes east again to Europe before moving on to its winter latitudes.

The exceptions to the rule are three, and two of these, the marbled godwit and the avocet, migrate to both ocean coasts, then southward, wintering east as well as west of their summer range. The third exception is the mountain plover. In one of the most rigid and least explicable of all migrations, this plover travels southwest 600 miles from its breeding grounds on the Great Plains, across the Rockies and the Coast Ranges of California; many of the arrivals in California then proceed south into northern Mexico, a region reached easily from the Great Plains without the trouble of negotiating two north-south ranges of high mountains. (Despite its name, which was given it only because the first specimen was taken in the Rocky Mountain foothills, this bird is not partial to mountains: it is a bird of short-grass country and would be better named the plains plover.) So fixed is it in its habits that though it breeds in Montana and Wyoming, it has never been recorded in the adjoining state of Idaho, nor in Nevada, nor in Oregon.[2]

Except for those species like the surfbird, wandering tattler and black turnstone which rarely or never leave the Pacific perimeter, the great majority of the Alaskan nesters travel a kind of transcontinental migration, flying southeast to Hudson Bay or the Atlantic Ocean before proceeding southward. This is markedly true of the western sandpiper, which breeds in northern and western Alaska and the Chukchi Peninsula of Siberia and winters chiefly in the Carolinas, and of the Eskimo curlew,

Hudsonian godwit and white-rumped sandpiper, which commonly perform the ocean flight from the Canadian Maritimes to South America.

Similarly, a number of buff-breasted sandpipers move east to Hudson Bay and onward, much less commonly, to the coast. From the coast the buff-breast apparently heads southwest again, across the Appalachians (it is not known to migrate through the South Atlantic states) to Central America, then southeast again to the Argentine. This odd zigzag route may be shared by the scattering of Baird's sandpipers that come east in the fall migrations, for their movements are also obscure once they leave the North Atlantic. There are few records of the Baird's sandpiper in the southeastern states and the West Indies.

Not all migrants, in other words, select the shortest route, much less the easiest. The Baird's sandpiper, quite apart from its zigzag course, migrates commonly along mountain chains in both the Andes and Rockies which would serve as barriers to ordinary birds; it has been seen flying busily along in the rarefied air at 13,000 feet. Similarly, the pectoral sandpiper has been recorded at 13,000 feet in Colorado and 12,000 feet in Argentina. The Mongolian plover which, like the rufous-necked sandpiper, crosses occasionally from Asia to breed on Alaska's Seward Peninsula, may nest at three miles above sea level in the Himalayas. (Godwits and curlews have been sighted at close to 20,000 feet in the same range, but these birds were presumably crossing the north-south barrier.)

While it may be that only the Baird's and pectoral sandpipers use the great cordilleras as a migration route, many wind birds migrate at high altitudes when conditions favor them. This would seem particularly logical for those that migrate after dark. The moon illumines coasts and rivers that serve as guidelines even in the night, and when the clouds close over, the night fliers may rise to high clear altitudes, their course oriented to the stars.

The sun is also used as a point of orientation—and certain shorebirds travel in the day as well as at night—but the majority of the smaller migrants prefer darkness. In daylight, when the sun consumes the precious energies needed for flight, it is more economical to feed and rest; at night, the air is apt to be more stable, and fewer predators are abroad. (Migrating birds, in the intensity of their journey, are notably unwary and may view with detachment small reductions of their number by hawk or prowling coon. But shorebirds can usually outmaneuver hawks in the rare instances when they cannot outfly them. On several occasions, I have watched a peregrine falcon in pursuit of shorebirds, but the only victim was a lone yellowlegs, caught low over the Sagaponack flats; it was knocked spinning to the ground like an old feathered pinwheel. The falcon, out of apathy or inexperience, did not turn fast enough to pin it down, nor did it pursue the wind bird very far when the latter pulled itself together and took off again with an impressive turn of speed.)

The night fliers rest well into the twilight, and most are aloft a short time after dark. Just before midnight, the migration reaches its peak; then a telescope trained on the moon can watch the steady stream across the sky. Before dawn, the tired birds have dropped onto other margins, hundreds of miles south. There they may rest a day, a fortnight or a month, depending on food, weather and the skies remaining between this point and their destination.

How birds orient themselves during migration remains the greatest of the unsolved questions in all avian studies. The young of the great distance fliers, starting southward without guidance on journeys of thousands of miles, must have at least an innate sense of primary direction. (A distinction should be made between directional sense, in which the bird, transplanted 500 miles west of its intended route, will theoretically arrive 500 miles west of its destination, and true homing ability, possessed by a few species, which would permit them to compensate for this displacement by the time they had arrived at their home latitudes. Most migrants do not seem to allow for wind displacement after their course is set; but they can apparently adjust the course, once arrived at a resting point, and have been observed[49] to return east or west again before proceeding southward.) Sense of direction, in adult birds, is probably supplemented by high-altitude search and by acute visual memory, which permits them to return to a given point once they arrive within a wide radius of the area. It is also supplemented by an internal timing mechanism, not yet understood, which gives the migrant some kind of azimuth bearing, using the sun or stars.

For reasons of food and prevailing winds, the golden plover which came up from the Argentine in spring by way of Peru and Yucatán, perhaps, or flew from Peru to the Gulf Coast and proceeded up the Mississippi Valley, does not return by the same route. Most, though not all, will complete an elliptical migration, the southbound arc of which takes them from their nesting grounds southeast across the continent to western New England and Delaware—a few go as far east as Nova Scotia and even Labrador—and on out across the open sea to South America; those that are seen at Sagaponack and elsewhere on the North Atlantic coast are probably deflected there by fog or storm.

The Eskimo curlew also made an elliptical or "loop" migration, and the Hudsonian godwit and white-rumped sandpiper make one still. But these three species may rest at Bermuda and in the Antilles, where the golden plover is quite rare: The first place that the plover turns up commonly is the Guianas. (The Eskimo curlew, on the other hand, was uncommon in Guiana, and it has been suggested[37] that this species flew a kind of "great circle" course, making its first landfall south of Cape San Roque in easternmost Brazil and possibly flying on southwest to the interior savannas without alighting.)

Yet even assuming an advanced navigational ability, how does one explain why many young golden plover, as if in defiance of the directional sense inherited from their parents, fail to follow the southeastward path that the adult birds have taken a few weeks earlier, choosing instead to take, in reverse, the path that brought the adults north? The choice of the interior route spares the young birds the awesome transoceanic flight of the adults, so that they may live to make that flight another year, but no known theory of migration can explain this choice except one so startling that to recognize it would be acknowledgment of an historic and continuing failure to comprehend the life dimensions: A few authorities, dissatisfied with all other explanations, have wondered if the young migratory bird *inherits* a topographic knowledge of the globe (an inherited knowledge of the constellations has already been established[81]), or at least of that segment of it that the bird must span each spring and autumn.[109]

The great overseas flights add the question of ocean navigation to the problem of orientation. Assuming that migrants use topographic features to refine a course based primarily on an inherited sense of direction, what landmarks prevent the wind bird which spans the gray trackless reaches of the sea from being carried far off course, or otherwise losing itself so irremediably that it must inevitably burn its strength and drop into the water, to flutter and blink and float a little before drifting down like a dead leaf into the void?

The ocean itself gives its mute signs—the cloud lines, for example, registering a change in air temperature and humidity in the region, say, of the Equatorial Current; or the long lines of sargassum weed and spindrift that betray the wind patterns; or the high cumulus which, looming over island outposts beyond the horizon, are visible to high-flying birds a hundred miles away. But all these signs presume fair weather and prevailing winds; if the voyager depends on them, then should it be caught at sea by heavy fog or overcast or even windlessness, it may be doomed. Considering the mixed conditions that the wind birds meet successfully in annual journeys of 15,000 miles or more, one should not underestimate their chances; yet good as a bird's orientation is, it cannot spare a large percentage of each species that one fatal mistake of navigation. Mere sense of direction seems inadequate. Without visual aids to correct its compass, a gale might cause the unlucky bird to miss or overshoot its target, as in the case of the ill-fated lapwings that flew to Canada.

And so there remains a mystery, and one pores anew over refuted theories based on bird sensitivity to the atmosphere's electric waves or to the guidelines of the earth's magnetic fields. Birds have been carried to far places in revolving cages or sent aloft with magnets fastened to their heads, without noticeable impairment of their homing ability. No experiment has ever proved that a bird can orient itself magnetically (although pigeons and many other birds have pectins or magnetic sensors in each eye),[20] but neither can the possibility be discarded, for the talent has been demonstrated in the otherwise ungifted common mud snail of our own Atlantic coast.[27]

The combination of abilities and experience doubtless differs from species to species. Certain sedentary birds have no homing ability whatsoever, while certain seabirds perform feats of navigation which confound the theorists, especially those who have left no place for metaphysics. None of the theories or combinations of theories presently considered reasonable provides an explanation of how a shearwater released in Venice, on a sea that none of its species ever visit, could and did return on an unfamiliar east-west bearing, across the European land mass in all likelihood, to its nesting ledge on a skerry in the Irish Sea, not in the season following but in 12½ days. There is no reason to suppose that a shorebird, put to an equivalent test, could not perform as well; and in regard to such a mystery, the exact scientists must do much better than they have done in the way of rigorous explanation if the rest of us, the awe-struck individuals who still glimpse fine, strange happenings through the screen of words and facts, are not to continue calling mystery by its proper name.

The departure of curlew from a given place often occurs just prior to a storm, and in ancient days, in England, the curlew's cry, the plover's whistle boded no man any good. Of the golden plover it was said in Lancashire that its sad whistle was the plaint of errant souls—not any old souls but the souls of those Jews who had lent a hand at the Crucifixion. In North England, curlews and whimbrels were called "Gabriel's hounds"; the name whimbrel comes from "whimpernel," which, in the Durham Household Book of 1530, refers to a habit attributed to it of houndlike whimperings.[5] Both birds were known as harbingers of death, and in the sense that they are birds of passage, that in the wild melodies of their calls, in the breath of vast distance and bare regions that attends them, we sense intimations of our own mortality, there is justice in the legend. Yet it is not the death sign that the curlews bring, but only the memory of life, of high beauty passing swiftly, as the curlew passes, leaving us in solitude on an empty beach, with summer gone, and a wind blowing.

Selected Bibliography

1. *Aegis.* Bel Air, Md., June 22, 1967.
2. American Ornithologists' Union. *The A.O.U. Check-list of North American Birds.* New York: American Ornithologists' Union, 1957.
3. Armstrong, E.A. *Bird Display and Behavior.* London: Lindsay Drummond, Ltd., 1947.
4. ——. *Bird Life.* New York: Oxford University Press, Inc., 1950.
5. ——. *Folklore of Birds.* Boston: Houghton Mifflin Company, 1959.
6. *Audubon Field Notes,* Vol. 18, No. 4, 1964.
7. Bannerman, David A. *Birds of the British Isles,* Vol. 9. London: Oliver & Boyd, Ltd., 1960.
8. Bent, Arthur C. *Life Histories of North American Shorebirds.* U.S. National Museum *Bulletin* No. 142, 1927.
9. Brandt, Herbert. *Alaska Bird Trails.* Cleveland: Bird Research Foundation, 1943.
10. ——. Cited in Bent. *See 8.*
11. Bull, John. *Birds of the New York Area.* New York: Harper & Row, Publishers, 1964.
12. Bullock, D.S. "North American Bird Migrants in Chile." *The Auk,* Vol. 66, pp. 351-54, 1949.
13. Cain, A.J. *Animal Species and Their Evolution.* New York: Harper & Row, Publishers, 1960.
14. Carr, Archie. *Ulendo.* New York: Alfred A. Knopf, Inc., 1964.
15. Chapman, Frank M. *Handbook of Birds of Eastern North America.* New York: D. Appleton & Company, 1909.
16. Cobb, S. "On the Angle of Cerebral Axis in the American Woodcock." *The Auk,* Vol. 76, pp. 55-59, 1959.
17. Collias, N.E. "The Development of Social Behavior in Birds." *Wilson Bulletin,* Vol. 58, pp. 1-41, 1952.
18. ——. "Evolution of Nest Building." *Natural History,* Vol. 74, pp. 40-47, 1965.
19. Conway, William G. "A Close Look at Argentine Wildlife." *Animal Kingdom,* Vol. 68, pp. 134-40, 1965.
20. ——. Correspondence and conversations with the author.

21. Cooke, Wells W. *Distribution and Migration of North American Shorebirds.* U.S. Biological Survey *Bulletin* No. 35, 1910.

22. Coues, Elliott. *Key to North American Birds.* 4th ed. Boston: L.C. Page & Company, 1892.

23. Darlington, P.J. *Zoogeography.* New York: John Wiley & Sons, Inc., 1959.

24. Darwin, Charles. Cited in Cain. *See 13.*

25. Dixon, Joseph. "The Home Life of the Baird Sandpiper." *The Condor,* Vol. 19, pp. 77-84, 1917.

26. ———. "The Surf-bird's Secret." *The Condor,* Vol. 29, pp. 3-16, 1927.

27. Dorst, Jean. *The Migration of Birds.* Boston: Houghton Mifflin Company, 1962.

28. Drury, W.H., Jr. "The Breeding Biology of Shorebirds on Bylot I., N.W. Territories, Canada." *The Auk,* Vol. 78, pp. 176-219, 1961.

29. Duffey, E., Creasey, N., and Williamson, K. "'Rodent-Run' Distraction Behavior of Certain Waders." *Ibis,* Vol. 92, pp. 27-33, 1950.

30. Emlen, J.T. "Flocking Behavior in Birds." *The Auk,* Vol. 69, pp. 160-70, 1952.

31. Fisher, James. Book review in *Ibis,* Vol. 97, No. 30, pp. 589-92, 1955.

32. Forbush, Edward Howe. *Game Birds, Wildfowl, and Shorebirds.* Boston: Massachusetts Board of Agriculture, 1912.

33. ———. *Birds of Massachusetts and Other New England States.* 3 vols. Boston: Commonwealth of Massachusetts, 1925-1929.

34. Gabrielson, Ira N., and Lincoln, Frederick C. *Birds of Alaska.* Harrisburg, Pa.: Stackpole Company, 1959.

35. Gilliard, E. Thomas. *Living Birds of the World.* New York: Doubleday & Company, Inc., 1958.

36. Gladkov, N.A. Cited by R.S. Palmer in conversation with the author.

37. Greenway, James C., Jr. *Extinct and Vanishing Birds of the World.* New York: American Committee for International Wildlife Protection, 1958.

38. Grinnell, George B. "Willets in Migration." *The Auk,* Vol. 33, pp. 198-99, 1916.

39. Hagar, J.A. "Nesting of the Hudsonian Godwit at Churchill, Manitoba." *The Living Bird*. Ithaca, N.Y.: Cornell University Press, 1970.

40. Hall, Henry M. *A Gathering of Shorebirds*. New York: The Devin-Adair Co., 1960.

41. Hamilton, W.J., III. "Aggressive Behavior in Migrant Pectoral Sandpipers." *The Condor*, Vol. 61, pp. 161-79, 1959.

42. Hesse, Richard, Allee, W.C., and Schmidt, Karl P. *Ecological Animal Geography*. New York: John Wiley & Sons, Inc., 1951.

43. Howard, Hildegarde. "Fossil Evidence of Avian Evolution." *Ibis*, Vol. 92, pp. 1-21, 1950.

44. Hubbs, Carl L. "The Rock Sandpiper, Another Northern Bird Recorded from the Cool Coast of Northwestern Baja California." *The Condor*, Vol. 62, pp. 68-69, 1960.

45. Hudson, W.H. *Birds of La Plata*. New York: E.P. Dutton and Co., Inc., 1920.

46. Huxley, Julian. Cited in Hall. *See 40*.

47. Knowles, E.H.M. "Nesting Habits of the Spotted Sandpiper." *The Auk*, Vol. 59, pp. 583-84, 1942.

48. Lack, David. "The Significance of Clutch Size." *Ibis*, Vol. 89, pp. 25-45, 1947.

49. ———. "Migration Across the Sea." *Ibis*, Vol. 101, pp. 374-99, 1959.

50. Laven, H. Cited in Welty. *See 109*.

51. Lorenz, Karl. "The Companion in the Bird's World." *The Auk*, Vol. 54, pp. 245-73, 1937.

52. Lowe, P.R. "Relations of Gruimorphae to Charadriimorphae." *Ibis*, Vol. 13, pp. 491-534, 1931.

53. Lowery, George M., Jr. "Evidence of Trans-Gulf Migration." *The Auk*, Vol. 63, pp. 175-211, 1946.

54. Mackay, G.H. Notes in *The Auk*, Vol. 13, pp. 80-81, 1896; Vol. 14, pp. 212-14, 1897; Vol. 15, pp. 52-53, 1898; Vol. 16, p. 180, 1899.

55. ———. Notes in *The Auk*, Vol. 14, pp. 212-14, 1897.

56. ——— Shooting Journal, 1865-1922. Cambridge, Mass.: privately printed, 1929.

57. Matthiessen, Peter. *Wildlife in America*. New York: The Viking Press, Inc., 1959.

58. Mayr, Ernst. "History of North American Bird Fauna." *Wilson Bulletin,* Vol. 58, pp. 3-41, 1946.

59. ——. "The Number of Species of Birds." *The Auk,* Vol. 63, pp. 64-69, 1946.

60. ——. "Speciation in Birds." *Proceedings,* Tenth International Ornithological Congress, pp. 91-131, 1950.

61. ——. *Animal Species and Evolution.* Cambridge, Mass.: Harvard University Press, 1963.

62. McCabe, T.T. "Types of Shorebird Flight." *The Auk,* Vol. 59, pp. 110-11, 1942.

63. Murie, Olaus J. "Nesting Records of the Wandering Tattler and Surf-bird in Alaska." *The Auk,* Vol. 41, pp. 231-37, 1924.

64. Murphy, Robert C. *Oceanic Birds of South America.* 2 vols. New York: American Museum of Natural History, 1936.

65. Nelson, Edward W. *Natural History Collections Made in Alaska.* Washington, D.C.: U.S. Department of Agriculture, 1877.

66. Nethersole-Thompson, C. and D. "Egg-shell Disposal by Birds." *British Birds,* No. 35, 1942.

67. Nice, Margaret M. "The Role of Territory in Bird Life." *Midland Naturalist,* Vol. 26, pp. 441-87, 1941.

68. ——. "Development of Behavior in Precocial Birds." *Transactions of the Linnaean Society,* No. 8, 1962.

69. Nichols, J.T., and Harper, F. "Field Notes on Some Long Island Shorebirds." *The Auk,* Vol. 33, pp. 237-55, 1916.

70. Nisbet T.C.T. "Wader Migration in North America and Its Relation to Transatlantic Crossings." *British Birds,* Vol. 52, pp. 205-15, 1949.

71. Noble, G.K., and Vogt, William. "Sex Recognition in Birds." *The Auk,* Vol. 52, pp. 278-86, 1935.

72. Palmer, Ralph S. Conversation with the author.

73. ——. Correspondence with the author.

74. ——. Species Accounts in G.D. Stout, ed., *The Shorebirds of North America.* New York: The Viking Press, Inc., 1967.

75. Parmelee, D.F. "Breeding Behavior of the Sanderling in the Canadian High Arctic." *The Living Bird.* Ithaca, N.Y.: Cornell University Press, 1970.

76. ——. Correspondence with the author, 1970-1972.

77. ——, Greiner, D.W., and Graul, W.D. "Summer Schedule and Breeding Biology of the White-rumped Sandpiper in the Central Canadian Arctic." *Wilson Bulletin,* Vol. 80, pp. 5-29, 1968.

78. —— and MacDonald, S.D. "The Birds of West-Central Ellesmere I. and Adjacent Areas." National Museum of Canada *Bulletin* No. 169, 1960.

79. ——, Stephens, H.A., and Schmidt, Richard H. "The Birds of Victoria I. and Adjacent Small Islands." National Museum of Canada *Bulletin* No. 222, 1967.

80. Peterson, Roger Tory. *A Field Guide to the Birds.* Boston: Houghton Mifflin Company, 1947.

81. —— and Fisher, James. *The World of Birds.* New York: Doubleday & Company, Inc., 1963.

82. Pettingill, O.S. "The American Woodcock." *Memoirs of the Boston Society of Natural History,* Vol. 9, pp. 167-391, 1936.

83. Pitelka, Frank A. "Geographic Variation and the Species Problem in the Shorebird Genus *Limnodromus.*" University of California *Publications in Zoology,* Vol. 50, pp. 1-108, 1950.

84. ——. "Number, Breeding Schedule, and Territoriality in Pectoral Sandpipers of Northern Alaska." *The Condor,* Vol. 61, pp. 233-64, 1959.

85. Portmann, Adolf. *Animal Camouflage.* Ann Arbor, Mich.: University of Michigan Press, 1959.

86. Pough, Richard H. *Audubon Water Bird Guide.* New York: Doubleday & Company, Inc., 1951.

87. Rand, Austin L. *American Water and Game Birds.* New York: E.P. Dutton & Co., Inc., 1956.

88. Recher, Harry F. "Some Aspects of the Ecology of Migrant Shorebirds." *Ecology,* Vol. 47, pp. 393-407, 1966.

89. Ridgway, R. *Birds of North and Middle America.* U.S. National Museum *Bulletin* No. 50, Part VIII, 1919.

90. Rothschild, M., and Clay, T. *Fleas, Flukes, and Cuckoos.* London: William Collins Sons & Co., Ltd., 1952.

91. Salomonsen, F. *Birds of Greenland.* Copenhagen: Munksgaard, 1950.

92. Schorger, A.W. "Jaçana Taken at Sea." *The Auk,* Vol. 63, p. 255, 1946.

93. Scott, Peter. *A Thousand Geese.* London: William Collins Sons & Co., Ltd., 1953.

94. Seebohm, Henry. *The Geographical Distribution of the Family Charadriidae, or the Plovers, Sandpipers, and Their Allies.* London, 1888.

95. Simmons, K.E.L. "The Nature of the Predator Reactions of Waders. . . ." *Behaviour,* Vol. 8, pp. 130-73, 1955.

96. Sprunt, Alexander, Jr., and Chamberlain, E.B. *South Carolina Bird Life.* Columbia, S.C.: University of South Carolina Press, 1949.

97. Stresemann, Erwin. Cited in Dorst. *See 27.*

98. Sutton, G.M. "Behavior of the Buff-breasted Sandpiper at the Nest." *Arctic,* Vol. 20, No. 1, pp. 3-7, 1967-1968.

99. ——. Memoirs of Carnegie Museum, Vol. XII, Part II, 1932.

100. Taverner, P.A. "The Distribution and Migration of the Hudsonian Curlew." *Wilson Bulletin,* Vol. 54, pp. 2-11, 1941.

101. Tinbergen, N. "The Behaviour of the Red-necked Phalarope . . . in Spring." *Ardea,* Vol. 24, pp. 1-42, 1935.

102. ——. "The Function of Sexual Fighting in Birds." *Bird Banding,* Vol. 7, pp. 1-8, 1936.

103. ——. *The Herring Gull's World.* London: William Collins Sons & Co., Ltd., 1953.

104. Tomkins, J.R. "Wilson's Plover in Its Summer Home." *The Auk,* Vol. 61, pp. 259-69, 1944.

105. Turner, E.L. "The Avocet at Home." *British Birds,* Vol. 14, pp. 194-202, 1921.

106. Vaurie, Charles. "Systematic Notes on Palearctic Birds. No. 53: Charadriidae: The Genera *Charadrius* and *Pluvialis.*" American Museum *Novitates,* No. 2177, 1964.

107. Vogt, William. "Notes on Behavior and Ecology of the Eastern Willet." *Proceedings of the Linnaean Society,* No. 49, pp. 8-42, 1937.

108. Webster, J. Dan. "The Breeding of the Black Oystercatcher." *Wilson Bulletin,* Vol. 53, pp. 141-56, 1941.

109. Welty, Joel C. *The Life of Birds.* New York: Alfred A. Knopf, Inc., 1963.

110. Wetmore, A. "Observations of the Birds of Argentina, Paraguay, Uruguay, and Chile." U.S. National Museum *Bulletin* No. 133, 1926.

111. Wilcox, Leroy. "A Twenty-Year Banding Study of the Piping Plover." *The Auk,* Vol. 76, pp. 129-52, 1959.

112. Williams, George G. "Do Birds Cross the Gulf of Mexico in Spring?" *The Auk,* Vol. 62, pp. 98-111, 1945.

113. ———. "Lowery on Trans-Gulf Migration." *The Auk,* Vol. 64, pp. 217-37, 1947.

114. Witherby, H.F., Jourdain, F.C.R., Ticehurst, N.F., and Tucker, B.W. *Handbook of British Birds,* Vol. 4. London: H.F. & G. Witherby, Ltd., 1940.

115. Wynne-Edwards, V.C. *Animal Dispersion in Relation to Social Behavior.* New York: Hafner Publishing Co., Inc., 1962.

Index

passenger pigeon, 18
Passeriformes, 93-94
Patagonia, 60, 103, 109
Peary, Admiral, 107
pectoral sandpiper, 31, 98-99; courtship
 pattern, 98; egg coloration, 113;
 migration, 144, 145, 146, 147; plumage
 coloration, 42; postnuptial flight, 134-
 136; protection of young, 129-130;
 redirection activity, 135; threat display,
 135; wing flight characteristics, 49; zigzag
 escape flight, 49
peep (small sandpiper), 90, 136, 137
pelican, 35
peregrine falcon, 68, 148
periwinkle, 98
Peru, 61, 149
Petersburg, Alaska, 141
phalarope, 84; courtship cycle, 104;
 incubation period, 115; northern, 39, 62,
 69-70, 91, 102-103, 104-105, 109, 111-
 112, 123, 133-134, 142; red, 34, 39, 62,
 70, 90, 113-114, 133-134, 142, 145; sex
 characteristics, 95; spin-and-dab
 technique, 39; Wilson's, 35, 39, 71, 96,
 104, 138, 145
Phalaropodidae, 85
Philomachus pugnax (*See* ruff)
Physa (bladder snail), 61
pigeon, 18, 150; passenger, 18
piping plover (*Charadrius melodus*), 19, 46,
 130; camouflage of, 41; chicks, 125-126;
 egg coloration, 113; fossil records, 45-46;
 injury-feigning, 122-123; migration, 58;
 nest intruders and, 121; nest site, 109;
 plumage and environment, 42;
 postnuptial flight, 136, 137
Pleistocene age, 61, 79, 81, 82
plover, 18, 25; bills, 36; black-bellied, 22, 31-
 32, 40, 41, 42, 61, 70, 78, 86, 121, 125,
 136, 138-139; black-breast, 20; breeding
 habits, 30; breeding range, 70; chicks,
 126; crab, 113; dotterel, 105, 119-120;
 egg coloration, 114; Egyptian, 110;
 feeding habits, 37-38; flock alightment,
 33; foot-patting technique, 38; golden,
 18, 20, 22, 34, 40, 42, 46-47, 50, 55-56,
 61, 71, 86, 90, 105, 108-109, 113, 122-
 123, 125, 129-130, 136, 138-139, 143,
 144, 149-152; habits and appearance, 25-
 26; Kittlitz's sand, 111; migration, 61-62,
 146, 150-151; Mongolian, 146;
 mountain, 25, 50, 66, 122, 123, 146; nest
 site, 109, 110; New Zealand shore, 74;
 piping, 19, 41, 42, 45-46, 58, 109, 113,
 121, 122-123, 125-126, 130, 136, 137;
 ringed, 42, 81, 103, 111, 122-123, 146;
 semipalmated, 42, 81, 113-114, 126-127,
 136, 137, 139; snowy, 22, 41, 42, 66, 71,
 81, 114; stone, 116; thick-knee, 25, 66,
 79, 119, 125, 128, 136; upland, 127;
 voice instinct, 94; white-fronted, 111;
 Wilson's, 35, 42, 59-60, 66, 96, 101, 102,
 114, 123, 139; wry-billed, 36
plumage, 40-43, 95, 137-138; purpose and
 function, 41-42
Pluvialis, 86
Pluvialis apricaria (greater golden plover),
 109
Point Barrow, 72, 73, 143-144
polymorphism, 99
Polynesia, 56
Poxabogue Pond, 17-18
pratincole, 25; injury-feigning, 123
preening habits, 31, 33
Presbyornis, 84
Pringle, James J., 67
promiscuity, 99-101; and hybridization, 101
ptarmigan, nest site, 109
Punta Piedras Blancas, 71
purple sandpiper, 47, 79-80; courtship, 97;
 egg coloration, 113; food hunting habits,
 38-39; migration, 66; nest intruders and,
 120; nest site, 109

quail, 46
Quebec, 72, 81

rail, 23, 24, 25
Raine, Walter, 81
raven, 34
Recurvirostridae, 36
red-backed sandpiper (*See* dunlin)
redirection activity, 135
red phalarope, 34; adaptive characteristics,
 39; animal food taken by, 34; breeding
 range, 70; egg coloration, 113-114; food
 hunting habits, 39; migration, 62, 142,
 145; postnuptial flight, 133-134;
 territoriality, 91
redshank, 143
reeve (*See* ruff)
Rensch's rule, 49
reproduction (*See* breeding cycle)
respiratory system, 46
Rhegminornis, 84-85
Rhode Island, 19
ringed plover: German name, 103; injury-
 feigning, 122-133; migration, 146; nest
 site, 111; plumage and environment, 42;